CONTEMPORARY'S

BRIDGES TO CRITICAL THINKING

READING
NONFICTION

READING LEVEL
CATEGORY
WORKBOOK AVAILABLE
TCHER. GUIDE AVAILABLE
PART OF A SERIES
OUT OF PRINT
CASSETTE AVAILABLE

CONTEMPORARY'S

BRIDGES TO CRITICAL THINKING

READING NONFICTION

BONNIE TIVENAN

Project Editor
Cathy Niemet

Consultants
Adele P. Barree
Learning Resources Department
Raritan Valley Community College
Somerville, New Jersey

Barbara Brodsky
Department of Biochemistry
Robert Wood Johnson Medical School
Piscataway, New Jersey

Kate Lindsey, M. Ed.
Reading Specialist
New Jersey Department of Corrections

CB

CONTEMPORARY
BOOKS

CHICAGO

Photo credits: p. 102—© Spencer Grant/ Photo
Researchers; p. 39—© Carl Frank/ Photo Researchers; pp.
24, 55, 59, 61, 75, 90—© AP/Wide World; p. 106—NASA

Library of Congress Cataloging-in-Publication Data

Tivenan, Bonnie.
    Bridges to critical thinking : reading nonfiction / Bonnie Tivenan.
        p.   cm.
    ISBN 0-8092-4193-5
    1. Critical thinking—Study and teaching.   2. Reading.   3. Reading
comprehension.   I. Title.
LB1590.3.T57   1991
372.4'1—dc20   91-10921
                                                                          CIP

Published by Contemporary Books, Inc.
Two Prudential Plaza, Chicago, Illinois 60601-6790
Manufactured in the United States of America
International Standard Book Number: 0-8092-4193-5

Published simultaneously in Canada by
Fitzhenry & Whiteside
195 Allstate Parkway
Markham, Ontario L3R 4T8
Canada

Editorial Director
Caren Van Slyke

Editorial
Pat Fiene
Sarah Schmidt
Sarah Conroy
Chris Benton
Joe Carrig
Eunice Hoshizaki

Editorial Assistant
Erica Pochis

Editorial Production Manager
Norma Fioretti

Production Editor
Jean Farley Brown

Cover Design
Lois Stein

Cover Illustrator
Kathy Petrauskas

Illustrator
Renée Mitchel Inc./Rachel Ann Shea

Art & Production
Syd Isham

Typography
Thomas D. Scharf

CONTENTS

BEGINNING 1

CHAPTER 1: GROUPING IDEAS .3
Warm-Up 4
Exercise 1 5
Writer's Workshop 6
Exercise 2 7
Mindstretcher 8
Paragraph: Are We Alone?: 9
Paragraph: An Amazing Scientist 10
Thinking About Thinking 12
Using What You've Learned .12
Writer's Workshop 13
Pass It On 13

CHAPTER 2: TOPIC SENTENCES AND DETAILS 14
Warm-Up 15
Exercise 1 16
Mindstretcher 16
Exercise 2 17
Exercise 3 19
Writer's Workshop 20
Check-Up 21
Paragraph: Potato Chips 22
Paragraphs: Iced Tea, Cereal 23
Paragraphs: Keeping a Light Bulb Glowing 24
Paragraphs: Rubber Tires, Penicillin 25
Using What You've Learned .26
Writer's Workshop 27
Thinking About Thinking 28
Pass It On 29

CHAPTER 3: MAIN IDEA SENTENCES 30
Warm-Up 31
How Articles are Organized .32
Exercise 1 34
Mindstretcher 35
Exercise 2 36
Writer's Workshop 37
Check-Up 38
Article: Amazon Adventure .39
Article: Moving Away from the Stone Age 41
Using What You've Learned .42
Thinking About Thinking 43
Writer's Workshop 44
Pass It On 44

CHAPTER 4: FOLLOWING SEQUENCE 45
Warm-Up 46
Exercise 1 47
Mindstretcher 48
Exercise 2: New Inventions 49
Writer's Workshop 50
Exercise 3: The Bermuda Triangle 51
Exercise 4 52
Writer's Workshop 53

Check-Up 53
Article: Dr. Martin Luther King, Jr. 55
Article: Jane Addams 58
Article: Cesar Chavez 61
Writer's Workshop 63
Thinking About Thinking 64
Using What You've Learned 65
Pass It On 65

CHAPTER 5: COMPARISON AND CONTRAST 66
Warm-Up 67
Exercise 1 68
Mindstrecher 69
Exercise 2 70
Exercise 3 71
Writer's Workshop 72
Article: Common Problems 73
Using What You've Learned 76
Article: Interview with Bob Harris about Japan 77
Writer's Workshop 79
Thinking About Thinking 80
Using What You've Learned 81
Pass It On 81

CHAPTER 6: CAUSE AND EFFECT .82
Warm-Up 83
Exercise 1 84
Exercise 2 85
Writer's Workshop 86
Mindstretcher 87
Exercise 3 88
Check-Up 89
Article: Fewer Factory Jobs .90
Writer's Workshop 92
Article: Father to Son 93
Article: A Service Job in Your Future? 94
Using What You've Learned 95
Thinking About Thinking 97
Pass It On 97

CHAPTER 7: OUTLINING AND SUMMARIZING 98
Warm-Up 99
Exercise 1: How Computers Have Changed 100
Mindstretcher 101
Exercise 2: Computers in the Future 102
Writer's Workshop 103
Exercise 3: Robots Now and in the Future 104
Check-Up 105
Article: The Future in Space 107
Article: Lasers 108
Writer's Workshop 110
Using What You've Learned 110
Thinking About Thinking 111
Pass It On 112

ANSWER KEY 113

Beginning

Put a check (✔) by the things you have done before.

- ☐ Made a list to organize the things you had to do
- ☐ Thought about the details in planning for a family vacation
- ☐ Read the directions for how to make a special dessert
- ☐ Compared the prices of clothes in several stores before you bought a new outfit
- ☐ Thought about the causes of a war and its effects on the people involved
- ☐ Outlined or wrote a summary of what you read in a textbook as a way to study for a test

If you have ever tried to do any of these things, you know that you had to be organized. You had to have a plan to carry out what you wanted to do.

Writers make a plan before they write. They choose a topic they want to write about and then list details that describe or explain the topic more fully.

In this book, *Reading Nonfiction*, you will read how writers develop sentences, paragraphs, and articles that include:

- a topic and details that describe the topic
- topic sentences and detail sentences (in paragraphs)
- main idea sentences, topic sentences, and detail sentences (in articles)
- sets of directions and time lines
- comparison and contrast—how things are the same or are different
- cause and effect—why things happen and their results
- an outline and a summary for various articles

You will learn how to take notes as you read so that you can be better prepared to study for tests. Taking notes will also help you learn and remember what you have read.

Each chapter has a **Tactics** section, where you will learn a skill and practice it. This is followed by a **Paragraphs** or **Articles** section, in which you will read selections and see how they have been organized.

In each chapter, the **Writer's Workshop** will give you a chance to write from your own experience about fun topics.

In the **Thinking About Thinking** sections, you will look at the differences between facts and opinions. You will decide if a statement can be proved true, or if it expresses how a person thinks or feels about a topic.

Before you read each longer article, there will be a prereading question that asks you to think about your prior experience, or what you already know about a topic. Then, as you read each article, you will be asked to stop and think about what you have read and to answer questions based on what you read. This is another way of taking notes as you read.

Each chapter has its own theme. The themes include the universe, inventions and discoveries, people who made a difference, prehistoric people, today's issues, jobs in the United States, and the future.

When you have finished *Reading Nonfiction*, you should feel a lot more confident as you read and take notes for your other classes. You will have learned how paragraphs and longer articles are organized. You will have learned how to read textbooks and other nonfiction materials with more ease. And you will have had fun while doing so.

1

Grouping Ideas

Have you ever made a list of things you wanted to remember to do?

Lists are useful aids. They help you put your thoughts in order and remember details. Stop for a moment and "organize yourself." List things that you need to do by the end of today.

Things to Do Today

1. _____

2. _____

3. _____

4. _____

Whenever you make a **list**, you are practicing a skill. You are organizing your ideas by putting similar ideas together in groups. In the list above, for example, all of the items have something in common. All of them are actions that you need to do by the end of the day.

Writers also use this listing skill. When they write, they group similar ideas together. In this chapter, you will use what you know about grouping ideas to read paragraphs. Reading and remembering information will be easier when you know how to find groups of ideas.

Tactics

WARM-UP

Directions: Use what you know about grouping ideas to add to the lists below.

Example:

Snacks
a) popcorn
b) corn chips
c) peanuts

d) *apples*

List 1: Jobs
a) carpenter
b) programmer
c) plumber

d) _____

List 2: Sports
a) tennis
b) baseball
c) basketball

d) _____

List 3: Singers
a) Madonna
b) Stevie Wonder

c) _____

d) _____

List 4: Holidays
a) Labor Day
b) Fourth of July

c) _____

d) _____

List 5: Money
a) penny
b) nickel

c) _____

d) _____

(Answers will vary.)

Topics and Details

What steps did you take when you made the five lists? You started with a general idea, or **topic**, like *snacks*. Then you were given words that "fit in with" or explained the topic, like *popcorn*, *corn chips*, and *peanuts*. Words and ideas that explain the topic are known as **details**.

Paragraphs follow the same pattern as lists. They also begin with a topic. Then they contain groups of sentences with details that "fit in with" or explain this idea. In the next exercise, you will find details that explain the topic of paragraphs.

EXERCISE 1

Directions: Each of the following paragraphs gives you information about a general idea, or topic. The topic has been underlined for you. As you read the paragraph, list the details that "fit in with" or explain the topic.

Example: Earth has <u>five oceans</u>. These oceans are the Atlantic, the Pacific, the Indian, the Arctic, and the Antarctic.

Topic: Five Oceans

a) Atlantic   **d)** Arctic
b) Pacific   **e)** Antarctic
c) Indian

1. <u>Five states</u> border the Pacific Ocean. Three western states—<u>Washington</u>, <u>Oregon</u>, and <u>California</u>—touch the Pacific Ocean. <u>Hawaii</u>, which consists of several islands, is surrounded by the Pacific Ocean. And the southern edge of <u>Alaska</u> borders the Pacific Ocean.

    Topic: Five States

    a) _____   **d)** _____

    b) _____   **e)** _____

    c) _____

2. Earth has <u>six continents</u>, or large areas of land. One of these continents is <u>North America</u>. Our country, the United States, is on this continent. A second continent is <u>Australia</u>. It is the only continent that is also one country. A third continent is <u>Antarctica</u>. It has the coldest weather of the six continents. Two other continents, <u>South America</u> and <u>Africa</u>, contain many developing nations. The sixth continent—<u>Eurasia</u>—has the most people.

Topic: Six Continents

a) _____ d) _____

b) _____ e) _____

c) _____ f) _____

(Answers are on page 113.)

Writer's Workshop

Directions: Lists can be about anything. Look at this list of topics and choose one that most interests you. Or think of your own topic. Write the topic on the blank line. Then write three details.

- Three Things I Would Do with a Million Dollars

- Three Things I Am Most Proud Of

- Three Famous People I Would Like to Meet

- Three Things I Would Like to Teach My Children

Topic:

_____

Details:

1. _____

2. _____

3. _____

(Answers will vary.)

EXERCISE 2

Directions: In each paragraph, details have been <u>underlined</u>. Then they have been put into a list. Look at the details in each list to see what they have in common. Then write the **topic** of the paragraph.

Example: The first men to land on the moon spent most of their time doing scientific work. They <u>collected samples of the moon's surface</u> to take back to Earth. They also <u>set up an instrument that measures solar wind</u>. And they <u>used a seismometer, another scientific instrument, to measure "moonquakes"</u>—movements in the moon's crust.

Details:

a) collected samples of the moon's surface
b) set up an instrument that measures solar wind
c) used a seismometer, another scientific instrument, to measure "moonquakes"

Topic: <u>scientific work done by men on the moon</u>

1. In our solar system, there are at least <u>nine planets</u>. The four planets closest to the sun are known as the inner planets. They are <u>Mercury</u>, <u>Venus</u>, <u>Earth</u>, and <u>Mars</u>. The five planets farther away from the sun are <u>Jupiter</u>, <u>Saturn</u>, <u>Uranus</u>, <u>Neptune</u>, and <u>Pluto</u>. They are known as the outer planets.

   Details:

a) Mercury	**d)** Mars	**g)** Uranus
b) Venus	**e)** Jupiter	**h)** Neptune
c) Earth	**f)** Saturn	**i)** Pluto

   Topic: _____

2. Our planet Earth has three layers. The outermost layer, or <u>crust</u>, is composed mainly of lightweight rock. Below the crust is the second layer, or <u>mantle</u>. This layer consists mostly of iron-rich rock. The third layer—the <u>core</u>—is made up of iron and nickel.

   Details:

a) crust	**b)** mantle	**c)** core

   Topic: _____

(Answers are on page 113.)

MINDSTRETCHER

Directions: Three words are "hidden" in the letters below. Find and underline the words.

```
t  j  k  p  c  r  b  v  t  e  n  n  i  s  a  z  e  r  u  q  m  x
e  n  p  o  q  z  d  t  x  z  c  s  y  t  r  n  a  x  b  c  c  z
x  r  m  a  u  p  b  n  z  f  o  o  t  b  a  l  l  u  p  p  y  k
z  x  m  s  o  c  c  e  r  d  b  a  m  l  z  p  m  b  n  q  a  s
```

Did you find the three words? If you had known that you were looking for the names of different sports, you might have found the words faster and more easily. If you did not find the three words before, try again now.

(Answers are on page 113.)

CHECK-UP

Part A

Directions: Answer these questions in your own words.

1. Name two ways in which paragraphs and lists are alike.

_____

2. What is a topic?

_____

3. What is a detail?

_____

Part B

Directions: Circle the letter of the title that tells the topic of the paragraph. (Details in the paragraph have been underlined.)

There are many heavenly bodies in our solar system. There are at least nine planets. Some of these planets have their own moons, just as Earth has its own moon. The planets and their moons circle around the sun—the main star in our solar system. There are also thousands of asteroids—small planetlike bodies.

a) The Sun and the Solar System
b) What Is in Our Solar System?

(Answers are on page 113.)

Paragraphs

GETTING READY

In this section of the chapter, you will read paragraphs about the universe. As you read each paragraph, apply what you have learned about grouping ideas. Ask yourself: What is the topic, or general idea explained in this paragraph? What are the details that explain the topic?

Do you think we are alone in the universe? Have you ever wondered if there is life on other planets? Scientists are looking for an answer to this age-old question.

Are We Alone?

Directions: Underline the letter of the title that tells the topic of each paragraph.

Paragraph 1

Many people are excited about the idea of life on other planets. Other people are frightened by this idea. People's hopes and fears do not change scientists' beliefs, however. In studying whether there is life on other planets, scientists look only at the facts.

a) Frightening Forms of Life in Outer Space
b) Scientists' Approach to Life in Outer Space

Paragraph 2

Some scientists believe that there may be life on other planets. They base this belief on the size of the universe. It is so large that it cannot be measured. We have hardly begun to explore the planets and other heavenly bodies in this limitless space. Given the size of the universe, some scientists think it is likely that planets other than Earth might support life. These scientists think that the same conditions that led to life on Earth may exist elsewhere in the universe.

a) Size of Universe Supports Idea of Life on Other Planets
b) Our Universe: Too Big to Be Measured Accurately

Paragraph 3

Some scientists believe that there may be life on other planets. But other scientists disagree. They point out several barriers to life in outer space. One problem is the atmosphere—the gases that surround other planets. Judging by the planets we have explored, the atmosphere in outer space could not support life as we know it. In addition, other planets are either too hot or too cold to support life. On an average day on Mercury, for example, the temperature ranges from 350° to −170° C.

a) Barriers to Life in Outer Space
b) Mercury: Land of Fire and Ice

(Answers are on page 113.)

Have you ever wondered how something began? Stephen Hawking is a scientist who has spent much of his life trying to answer questions about how the universe got started.

An Amazing Scientist

Directions: Answer each question after you read each part of this article.

Many scientists have studied outer space and the universe. One of the most amazing of these scientists is a man named Stephen Hawking. As you read about Stephen Hawking, notice that the titles tell you the topic of each paragraph. Look for details that explain each of these topics.

Hawking's Physical Problems

Stephen Hawking, one of the most famous scientists in the world, has several disabilities. He cannot move his arms and legs. In fact, he can move only his eyes and three fingers on his right hand. He has difficulty swallowing liquids, and he cannot talk. Stephen Hawking has Lou Gehrig's disease, an illness that destroys the nervous system.

Two details of Hawking's physical problems are listed. Add two more details to the list.
a) Lou Gehrig's disease attacked Hawking's nervous system.
b) Hawking cannot move his arms and legs.

c) _____

d) _____

Hawking's Daily Life

In many ways, Stephen Hawking lives a normal life. He has friends. He travels, and he works. But in other ways, Hawking's life is not like other people's. To get around, he drives a motorized wheelchair. To talk, he uses a special computer with a voice machine attached to it. The computer puts words on a screen, and Hawking selects which words he wants. Then the computer sends these words to the voice machine. There is a six-second delay, or gap, between words that the voice machine "speaks."

Two details of Hawking's daily life are listed. Add two more details from the paragraph to the list.

a) Hawking has friends.
b) Hawking travels and works.

c) _____

d) _____

Big Bang Theory

In 1970, Hawking used math to show that the big bang theory could be true. The big bang theory is a scientific explanation for how the universe might have begun. Many scientists believe that long ago all matter and energy was squeezed into a very small space. They are not sure, but they believe the space may have been no larger than a basketball. Then, twenty trillion years ago, this matter and energy exploded. It became the stars, planets, and everything else that is now the universe.

Two details about the big bang theory are listed. Add two more details from the paragraph to the list.

a) The big bang theory explains how the universe might have begun.
b) Long ago, all matter and energy was squeezed into a small space.

c) _____

d) _____

Hawking's New Theory

Although Stephen Hawking used math to prove the big bang theory, he no longer is satisfied with the theory. Today, he does not believe that it explains how the universe began. Stephen Hawking is now working on another theory. According to this new theory, the universe cannot be measured because it has no borders or edges. He also believes that the universe is infinite; that means the universe had no beginning and has no end.

A detail about Hawking's new theory is listed. Add another detail from the paragraph to the list.

a) Hawking believes that the universe cannot be measured.

b) _____
_____

(Answers are on page 113.)

Thinking ABOUT Thinking

Scientists gather and study facts about the world around us. **Facts** are pieces of information that can be proved true. Facts are supported by research and evidence.

Opinions are personal beliefs. Opinions are different from facts because they cannot be proved true. While facts are the same for everybody, opinions are not. Opinions can vary from person to person.

Directions: Underline the correct answers.

1. There are six continents on Earth.
   a) Can this statement be proved with evidence?
      yes   no
   b) Is this statement a fact or an opinion?
      fact   opinion

2. North America is the most beautiful continent.
   a) Can this statement be proved with evidence?
      yes   no
   b) Is this statement a fact or an opinion?
      fact   opinion

(Answers are on page 113.)

USING WHAT YOU'VE LEARNED

Directions: Answer the questions in your own words.

1. For many years, people have dreamed of starting colonies on other planets. If the United States were to start a settlement on Mars, would you volunteer to go? Why or why not?

   _____

   _____

2. In your opinion, what is Stephen Hawking's greatest success? Explain why you feel as you do.

   _____

   _____

(Answers will vary.)

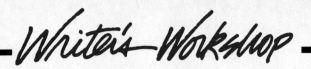

Directions: Fill in the details in this paragraph. Think about someone you know or have read about who has overcome a serious problem.

A person I know, named _____, has overcome a serious

problem. The problem that was overcome was _____.
To overcome this problem, the person took the following steps:

_____

_____

_____

(Answers will vary.)

PASS IT ON

Some people say that we are living in the Information Age. Through computers, fax machines, videos, television, and other media, people share interesting and important information.

Recall some interesting information that you learned in this chapter. Do someone a favor and pass the information on. Tell the other person what you learned.

1. What new information that you've learned in this chapter will you pass on?

_____

_____

2. Who will you pass this information on to?

_____

(Answers will vary.)

2

Topic Sentences and Details

What kinds of TV shows are your favorites? List the kinds that you find the most interesting.

_____

_____

_____

_____

Imagine that you are a writer for a TV guide. You are writing about a particular **topic**, or general subject. Your subject is "popular kinds of TV shows." If you write about sports shows, detective shows, comedy shows, or game shows, those are **details** that give some information about your topic.

In this chapter, you will learn how writers begin with a topic sentence and support it with details when they write paragraphs. You will also read about some inventions and discoveries. Once you learn how to look for topic sentences and details, you will understand more of what you read.

Tactics

WARM-UP

Directions: Read each list of words. <u>Underline</u> the topic, or general subject, that tells what the details in each list are about.

Example: walking
bicycles
trains
<u>transportation</u>
cars

> This is the general topic. All of the rest are *specific types* of transportation.

1. green
yellow
orange
colors
red

2. farmers
factory workers
jobs
nurses
secretaries

3. mystery
books
drama
romance
comic

4. jazz
blues
rock
music
country and western

(Answers are on page 114.)

Topic Sentences and Details   **15**

Finding a Topic

In the warm-up exercise, you were asked to find the topic within each list. The topic told what the rest of the list was about. In the next exercise, you will look at each list and decide what the topic is.

EXERCISE 1

Directions: Read these lists. Then write the topic of each list.

Example: winter
spring
summer
fall
Topic: _seasons_

1. farm
   factory
   office
   Topic: _____

2. T-shirt
   dress
   suit
   Topic: _____

3. condo
   apartment building
   house
   Topic: _____

4. Spanish
   English
   Russian
   Topic: _____

(Answers are on page 114.)

MINDSTRETCHER

When they write, writers may first think of a general topic. Then they narrow it down to a more specific topic so they can focus their ideas.

Directions: Each of these lists has two topic words. The one that is too general is in **bold type**. <u>Underline</u> the more specific topic in each list.

Example: Sting   **people**   Prince   Cher   <u>singers</u>
1. parrot   sea gull   birds   **animals**   pigeon
2. pie   **food**   desserts   cakes   ice cream   cookies
3. relatives   mother   father   **people**   brother   sister
4. poodle   collie   sheepdog   dogs   **animals**

(Answers are on page 114.)

Finding the Topic Sentence

When you are asked the question "What is the paragraph about?" you may find the answer in the **topic sentence**. A topic sentence makes a statement about a topic. It tells what point the writer wants to make about a topic.

Example:
Topic: Inventions
Topic Sentences: Inventions can be fun.
Inventions are often rewarding.
Many people have made useful inventions.

EXERCISE 2

Directions: Underline the topic sentence that tells what each paragraph is about. All the other sentences in each paragraph contain details that explain the topic sentence.
Note: Sometimes the topic sentence is found at the beginning of the paragraph. Sometimes it is found at the end.

Example: The First Vacuum Cleaner

<u>One of the first household vacuum cleaners was invented by a janitor named James Murray Spangler in 1908.</u> Spangler was using a carpet sweeper to clean some carpets in a store. But the air was so thick with dust that he suffered from bad coughing spells. Spangler built a vacuum cleaner from a fan motor, a soap box, a broom handle, and a pillowcase. The machine worked!

Earmuffs

On a winter day in 1873, fifteen-year-old Chester Greenwood was ice-skating on a pond near his home in Maine. Chester's ears began to turn red, and then blue, and then to sting because of the cold winds, since he was not wearing a hat. Chester decided to do something to keep his ears warm. He went home and twisted some wire into two loops. His grandmother sewed heavy cloth onto each loop. Then he connected the two loops with a metal band that would fit over his head. Now he could keep his ears warm. At age 18, Chester Greenwood got a patent for his invention—earmuffs.

Braille

In 1824, at age 15, a blind French boy named Louis Braille invented a system so that blind people could read. He wanted to read as easily as people who could see. Braille got his idea from a code used by the French army. The code was made up of a combination of punch marks made in paper. Braille worked on his idea for two years. Finally, he had a system of six raised dots that could be combined in sixty-three different ways to make letters, words, and numbers. Now blind people could read quickly by running their fingertips across the dots on a page. Today his system is still used all over the world.

(Answers are on page 114.)

Finding Details

Most paragraphs in Exercise 2 began with a topic sentence. All the other sentences gave **details** that explained what the topic sentence was about.

Read this sample paragraph. Under the paragraph is a diagram. The diagram shows how the topic sentence is related to the other sentences.

Example: The Cherokee Writing System

[1]Sequoya invented a system of writing for his Native American tribe, the Cherokees. [2]He did this so that they could have their own language to write with. [3]Sequoya worked on this writing system for 12 years and completed it in 1812. [4]As a result, the Cherokees used this writing system to publish books and newsletters in their own language.

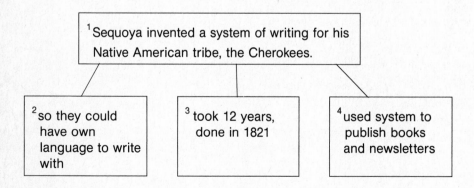

EXERCISE 3

Directions: Now make your own diagram to show how the topic sentence relates to the other sentences. You can write phrases based on the sentences.

Roller Skates

[1]In 1863, James Plimpton of Massachusetts invented a pair of roller skates. [2]He put rubber cushions between the foot plates and the axles of a pair of shoes that had four wheels on the bottom. [3]The cushions allowed motion between the parts of the wheels. [4]Now a skater could shift his weight and use motion to steer in the direction he wanted to go. [5]Roller skating as a leisure activity soon swept across the nation.

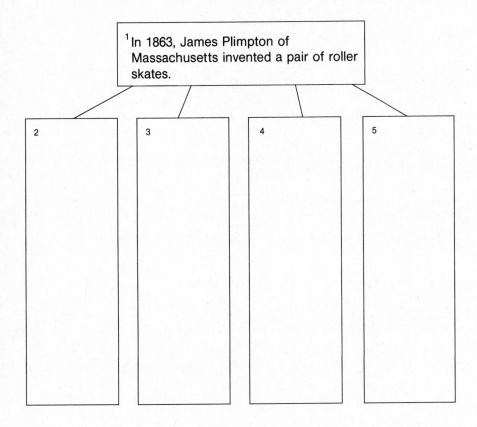

[1]In 1863, James Plimpton of Massachusetts invented a pair of roller skates.

2

3

4

5

(Answers are on page 114.)

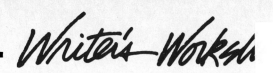

Directions: In this Writer's Workshop, you will name
don't like to do. Then you will think up an invention
for you. First read this sample.

Sample problem: I hate homework.
Sample invention: homework machine
Topic sentence: I have invented the ideal time-saver
machine.
Supporting details:

1. I got tired of writing my homework every night, s
   machine.

2. I programmed a computer to read my mind.

3. Each night, I look at my computer, giving it my full attention.

4. Then the computer begins typing out everything that I am thinking.

5. Before I have time to worry about it, the computer prints out a
   homework assignment that I can hand in the next day.

Now you write about your problem and invention.

Your problem: _____

Your invention: _____

Topic sentence: _____

Supporting details: _____

_____

_____

_____

_____

_____

_____

(Answers will vary.)

CHECK-UP

Directions: Think about the important points made in this chapter. Write your answers on the lines.

1. When you find the topic in a paragraph, what question do

   you answer? _____

2. Underline the topic sentence in the following paragraph.

   There is an interesting story about how the first sandwich
   was created. The fourth earl of Sandwich, an English
   nobleman in the 1700s, was a known gambler. One night,
   he was hungry but did not want to take time to eat. During
   a card game, he ordered a servant to bring him some meat
   and two pieces of bread. He slapped the meat and bread
   together and created a sandwich. Now he could eat a
   sandwich with one hand and hold his cards with the other.
   The sandwich became a very popular meal from then on.

3. Reread the paragraph. Write the topic sentence. List the
   details that are given in the paragraph.

   Topic sentence: _____

   _____

   Details: _____

   _____

   _____

   _____

   _____

   _____

   _____

   _____

(Answers are on page 114.)

Paragraphs

GETTING READY

You have learned about finding a topic and making a list of details that explain or describe the topic. Now you will practice finding the **topic sentence** of a paragraph. Then you will look for the **details** that explain the topic sentence. Each paragraph will tell about how a new invention or discovery was made.

Have you ever created a new recipe to share with your friends? Here's how a few common foods and drinks were created.

Directions: Add details from the paragraph on the lines.

Potato Chips

Potato chips were created by accident in 1853 by George Crum. George was a chef in a restaurant in Saratoga, New York. He served french fries to a guest, who complained that the fries were too thick, too soggy, and not salty enough. In anger, George cut the potatoes into paper-thin slices. He soaked the slices in water for 30 minutes; then he cooked them and added salt. He served the potatoes cold and crisp. The customers loved this tasty new treat. The first potato chips were called "Saratoga chips," named after the town that George came from.

Topic sentence: *Potato chips were invented by accident in 1853 by George Crum.*

Details: _____

_____

_____

_____

_____

_____

_____

Iced Tea

Iced tea was invented by accident in the early 1900s. Richard Blychenden worked at the St. Louis Exposition as a tea salesman. He was trying to sell hot cups of tea, but the tea was so hot that no one would drink it. Richard poured the hot tea over some ice chips in a cup. His business quickly grew. Hundreds of people came to his booth to try his new invention—iced tea.

Topic sentence: *Iced tea was invented by accident in the early 1900s.*

Details: _____

_____

_____

_____

_____

Cereal

Drs. John and Will Kellogg ran a health clinic in Battle Creek, Michigan. They opened a food laboratory to test healthy new breakfast foods. The doctors were trying to create a low-starch, whole-grain wheat bread. When the doctors were called out of the lab for several hours, the wheat they were boiling became soggy. They pressed the wheat under flat rollers. When it dried, instead of being a flat sheet, the wheat broke up into separate crispy flakes. They poured milk over the flakes and called their new creation "cereal." So Drs. John and Will Kellogg created breakfast cereal by accident in the late 1800s.

Topic sentence: *So Drs. John and Will Kellogg created breakfast cereal by accident in the late 1800s.*

Details: _____

_____

_____

_____

_____

_____

_____

_____

(Answers are on page 114.)

Looking at Inventions

Sometimes inventors work for years and years to make a discovery. At other times, they are lucky and find out by accident how something works. The inventions you will read about were discovered either by accident or after many years of effort. Look for the topic sentences and the details as you read these paragraphs.

Have you ever discovered something by accident, or worked for a long time to make something work? These inventors did both.

Directions: Write the topic sentence and the details of the following three paragraphs on the lines.

Keeping a Light Bulb Glowing

In 1879, Thomas Edison found a way to keep a light bulb glowing for a long period of time. He had worked on this idea for 15 months before he found a solution. Edison wanted to find the right filament, or part that glows inside the light bulb. Finally, he tried charred cotton thread. It glowed for 40 hours. He had found his solution.

Topic sentence: _____

_____

Details: _____

_____

_____

_____

_____

_____

Rubber Tires

In 1839, Charles Goodyear was looking for a way to make rubber that could be used for tires. Goodyear mixed sulfur and white lead with gum rubber. He found that the rubber got too soft and sticky in heat and too hard and stiff in cold. By accident, some of the mixture spilled onto a hot stove. When the rubber cooled, it was a tough material that stayed the same in both hot and cold temperatures. Goodyear used this rubber to make the tires we now use on our cars, trucks, buses, and airplanes.

Topic sentence: _____

_____

Details: _____

_____

_____

_____

_____

_____

_____

_____

_____

Penicillin

In 1928, Alexander Fleming discovered penicillin by accident. He was studying bacteria and found some mold in one of the cultures[1] he was growing in the lab. Fleming found that bacteria did not grow in the culture that had the mold in it. He grew the mold in fluid and found that it had a substance in it that could kill many kinds of common bacteria. He tested this mold on mice, rabbits, and human cells, and none of the animals or cells were harmed. Fleming called this medicine *penicillin*. It was used during World War II to treat wounded soldiers. Penicillin has been used ever since then to fight bacteria.

Topic sentence: _____

_____

Details: _____

_____

_____

_____

_____

_____

_____

[1] Fluid or solid that bacteria is grown in to be studied.

(Answers are on page 115.)

USING WHAT YOU'VE LEARNED

Part A

Directions: These are four steps an inventor might take to solve a problem and create a new invention. Match these four steps with the things Edison did to keep a light bulb glowing.

Inventor's Steps

_____ **1.** An inventor chooses a problem he wants to solve.

_____ **2.** He keeps working at the problem for however long it takes to solve the problem.

_____ **3.** He records all his ideas and findings in a notebook as he is working.

_____ **4.** He records his final solution and describes what finally made his invention work.

Edison's Steps

a) Edison wrote down all his findings in a notebook as he worked.

b) Edison wanted to find a way to keep a light bulb glowing.

c) Edison recorded his final solution—that charred thread would keep glowing for 40 hours.

d) Edison worked on finding the right kind of filament for 15 months.

(Answers are on page 115.)

Part B

Directions: These are five steps Alexander Fleming took to invent penicillin. Number the steps in order.

_____ Fleming tested the mold on animal and human cells and he found that the cells were not harmed.

_____ When Fleming was studying bacteria, he found some mold growing in one of the cultures.

_____ Fleming called the medicine *penicillin.*

_____ Fleming grew the mold in fluid and found that the substance could kill bacteria.

_____ Penicillin has been used ever since to fight bacteria.

(Answers are on page 115.)

Now you have read about how several inventions were made. In this Writer's Workshop, it is your turn to become an inventor.

Directions: The topics listed are some common household items that you might use every day. Think of three new and different ways that each item can be used. Write these details on the lines.

Example: new ways to use clothespins
a) to hang up wet photos to dry after they have been developed
b) to keep open bags of potato chips tightly closed and fresh
c) to make kids' toys, like butterflies or stick people, by decorating them with markers

1. new ways to use an egg carton

a) _____

b) _____

c) _____

2. new ways to use paper plates

a) _____

b) _____

c) _____

3. new ways to use drinking straws

a) _____

b) _____

c) _____

(Answers will vary.)

Thinking ABOUT Thinking

What is the difference between a **fact** and an **opinion**? A *fact can* be proved true. Sentences that are facts often have dates, times, or names of people or places that can be checked. An *opinion cannot* be proved. It states a feeling. An opinion sentence often contains a word like *most, all, everybody, better,* or *best*.

Part A

Directions: Read each sentence. <u>Underline</u> the part of each sentence that can be checked and proved as a *fact*.

Example: In <u>1879</u>, <u>Thomas Edison</u> found that charred cotton thread would keep a light bulb glowing for <u>40 hours</u>.

1. George Crum invented potato chips in Saratoga, New York, in 1853.

2. Iced tea was first served at the St. Louis Exposition in the early 1900s.

3. John and Will Kellogg invented cereal by accident in the late 1800s.

4. In 1839, Charles Goodyear created the correct mixture to make rubber that could be used for tires.

5. Penicillin was discovered by Alexander Fleming in 1928.

Part B

Directions: Read each sentence. <u>Underline</u> the part of each sentence that shows it is an *opinion*.

Example: Thomas Edison was the <u>greatest</u> American inventor of his time.

1. Hot potatoes taste better than cold potatoes.

2. Most people like to eat cereal for breakfast.

3. Goodyear makes the best tires for cars.

4. Everybody enjoys eating Kellogg's cornflakes.

5. All Americans like potato chips more than french fries.

(Answers are on page 115.)

PASS IT ON

You have learned some ways in which inventions were created. Common things like cereal, rubber tires, iced tea, and potato chips were created by inventors who wanted to solve a problem. They worked on their ideas, recorded their findings, and found a solution. In doing this, they made new inventions.

Do yourself a favor. Pass on some new information you learned in this chapter. By telling someone else what you learned, you will remember the details better.

1. What new information that you've learned in this chapter will you pass on?

_____

_____

_____

_____

_____

_____

_____

_____

2. Who will you pass this information on to?

_____

(Answers will vary.)

3
Main Idea Sentences

Have you ever tried to plan a wedding or a big family party? If so, you might have made lists like the following, so that you didn't forget any details. Look at each heading and fill in a few more items on each list.

Guests	Florist Shops	Food Stores
Bob and Jean Lee	The New Leaf	Good Foods

When you are planning a big party, you need to make several lists to include all the details. In the same way, writers need to use more than one paragraph when they write about more than one idea.

A series of paragraphs is called an **article**. Every article has a **main idea sentence** that tells what the article is about. The main idea sentence is usually found at the beginning of the article, but sometimes it is found at the end. Keep this in mind as you read articles.

In this chapter, you will see how paragraphs and articles are alike. You will also read articles about prehistoric people and how they lived.

Tactics

WARM-UP

If all the articles in a magazine were put into one big list of titles, it would take a long time to find the article you were looking for. So the table of contents has categories like *Travel*, *People*, and *Style*. The articles about these topics are listed under each category heading.

Example: *Travel*

How to See Europe on $50 a Day
San Francisco, the City on the Bay

Directions: Find the two articles that fit into each category. Write the letters on the lines.

_____ **1.** Fashion

_____ **2.** Finance

_____ **3.** Family

a) Ten Ways to Boost Your Child's Self-Esteem

b) Miniskirts Are In

c) IRAs—A Good Investment?

d) Fun Vacations with Children

e) Do You Need Life Insurance?

f) How to Tie a Scarf in 50 Ways

(**Answers are on page 115.**)

Main Idea Sentences

How Articles Are Organized

A paragraph usually begins with a topic sentence that tells what the paragraph will be about. An article, made up of several paragraphs, usually begins with an opening paragraph which includes a main idea sentence that tells what the whole article will be about.

These diagrams show you how paragraphs and articles are alike.

A paragraph contains sentences with details that explain the topic sentence. And an article contains paragraphs with details that explain the main idea sentence.

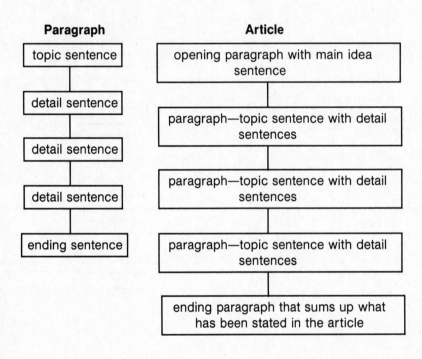

Paragraph	Article
topic sentence	opening paragraph with main idea sentence
detail sentence	paragraph—topic sentence with detail sentences
detail sentence	paragraph—topic sentence with detail sentences
detail sentence	paragraph—topic sentence with detail sentences
ending sentence	ending paragraph that sums up what has been stated in the article

Sample Paragraph

Fossils, which are imprints of living things on rocks, have helped scientists learn what our world was like millions of ← topic sentence
years ago. Scientists have studied fossilized teeth and bones of people who died long ago. They have also studied fossils of plants from prehistoric times. And they have studied some fossilized footprints. ← detail sentences
From these studies, they have made some good guesses about what earlier times may have been ← ending sentence
like.

Sample Article

Fossils, which are imprints of living things on rocks, have helped scientists learn what our world was like millions of ← main idea sentence
years ago. Scientists have studied fossilized teeth and bones, fossilized plants, and some footprints to draw their ← opening paragraph
conclusions about what life was like at that time.

Because of their hardness, teeth and bones may be the only parts of ancient humanlike bodies that have been preserved. From scratch marks on the teeth, scientists can tell that ← detail paragraph
prehistoric people ate meat. They also ate roots and plants.

By studying the imprints of plants on rocks, scientists have learned what the climate was like in prehistoric times. They ← detail paragraph
also know the types of plants these prehistoric creatures ate.

By studying some footprints found in volcanic ash, scientists ← detail paragraph
have learned in what areas these people lived. They also have an idea of what size these people were.

As you can see, these findings gave the scientists a lot of clues about how prehistoric people lived. Scientists learned what
kinds of foods they ate, where they lived, the type of climate ← ending paragraph
they lived in, and what size the people were. Thus scientists have made some links to our distant past.

EXERCISE 1

Directions: The main idea sentence of the following article has been underlined. Underline the topic sentence in each of the other paragraphs in the article.

Scientists have learned a lot about early forms of humanlike creatures (called *hominids*) by finding parts of a skeleton from that time. These creatures lived more than 4 million years ago in Ethiopia. They walked upright, but also did some tree climbing. They were much smaller than humans are today.

A scientist discovered parts of a prehistoric female skeleton. He named the skeleton Lucy. When her bones were put together, 40 percent of her skeleton was there. He rebuilt the rest of the skeleton to get an idea of the shape and size of her frame. By looking at the shape of Lucy's leg and hipbones, he could tell that she walked upright.

Looking at the curve of her toe bones, the scientist could tell that Lucy had done some tree climbing. He guessed that she walked on the ground during the day looking for food. And at night, she probably climbed into a tree so that she would be safe from her enemies.

By rebuilding the missing parts of Lucy's skeleton, the scientist learned her height. She was about 3½ feet tall. This means she was much shorter than women are today.

Scientists are very excited that this skeleton has been found. They can learn so much about prehistoric creatures who walked the earth before us by studying the clues these creatures left behind.

(Answers are on page 115.)

MINDSTRETCHER

The title of an article tells what the whole article will be about. The title should not be too narrow, telling about only part of the topic. Nor should the title be too broad, or general.

Directions: These are the opening paragraphs of longer articles. Write **BT** before the best title, **TN** before the title that is too narrow, and **TB** before the title that is too broad.

Example: People living today still have some of the same needs as people who lived 40 thousand years ago. People still like to live in groups. They still use tools to make and repair things. People still need to obtain food to survive.

_____TB_____ **a)** How People Lived in the Past

_____TN_____ **b)** How People Used Tools

_____BT_____ **c)** Similar Needs of People Today and in the Distant Past

1. People's language ability has grown a lot in the past several thousand years. The first people only made sounds and hand gestures to talk with each other. Gradually, people made up words to express their feelings, needs, and ideas. Today, people's ability to speak many languages has become very highly developed.

   _____ **a)** Sounds and Hand Gestures among Early People

   _____ **b)** How People's Language Ability Has Grown and Developed

   _____ **c)** How People Express Their Feelings, Needs, and Ideas

2. Thousands of years ago, males and females depended on one another for survival. Work was divided among men and women depending on their skills, strength, and abilities. This working together led to close family relationships.

   _____ **a)** How Work Was Divided among Men and Women in the Past

   _____ **b)** People's Skills, Strength, and Abilities

   _____ **c)** How Close Family Relationships Grew among People in the Past

(Answers are on page 115.)

EXERCISE 2

Directions: Read the entire passage. Underline the main idea sentence in the first paragraph that tells what the whole article will be about. The topic sentences of the other paragraphs have been underlined for you.

Scientists know a lot about the Neanderthals from studying their fossilized skulls, skeletons, and tools. The first fossils were discovered in the Neander Valley in Germany, and so scientists named this group of people the Neanderthals. Scientists know where and when the Neanderthals lived and what they looked like. They know the types of animals the Neanderthals hunted, the types of homes they built, and the types of clothing and decorations they made.

By studying the parts of skeletons that have been found, scientists have discovered where and when the Neanderthals lived and what they looked like. Scientists believe that the Neanderthals may have lived near the end of the Ice Age about 35,000 to 85,000 years ago. They probably lived in Europe, western Asia, and northern Africa. A strongly built, muscular people, they were short and stout. They had heavy brow ridges, large teeth, and small cheekbones.

Scientists also know the types of animals the Neanderthals hunted, the types of homes they built, and the types of clothing and decorations they made. The Neanderthals hunted mammoths (huge, hairy elephants with long curved tusks) and caught fish. Some Neanderthals used the mammoth bones to make huts, which they covered with skins and moss to keep out rain and cold winds. With the mammoth bones they also made needles to sew with and necklaces and beads to wear. From the mammoth hides they made shoes and clothing to protect themselves from the extremely cold weather. Most Neanderthals were cave dwellers who were very skilled at hunting and building fires.

The Neanderthals made more elaborate tools than earlier groups of people had made. They used flint, a hard rock, and attached it to pieces of bone or wooden handles to make several types of tools. They used these flint tools for hunting, cutting, repairing, and making things.

You may wonder why the Neanderthals no longer exist. It is believed that they could not withstand the hardships of the Ice Age. Although the Neanderthals lived thousands of years ago, scientists in our time have discovered many clues left behind by this early group of people that tell us how they lived.

(Answer is on page 115.)

Writer's Workshop

Directions: Read the detail sentences below. Then write a main idea sentence to introduce what each article will be about. (Only the opening paragraph of each article is shown here.)

Article 1: Early Cave Paintings

Main Idea Sentence: _____

_____

_____

_____

To make colorful paintings, primitive people used Earth's many colors and mixed them with water. They used either their fingers or the ends of twigs to paint with. These paintings, found on cave walls, tell us what was important to these early people.

Article 2: The First Farmers

Main Idea Sentence: _____

_____

_____

_____

As the Ice Age came to an end, primitive people began to farm the land for the first time. They collected wild grasses. They learned to keep animals. They also discovered how to grow crops.

(Answers are on page 116.)

CHECK-UP

Directions: Answer each question. Look back at the chapter if you do not know an answer.

1. Which two kinds of sentences are found in a paragraph?

_____

_____

2. Which three kinds of sentences are found in an article?

_____

_____

_____

3. What does the main idea sentence in an article do?

_____

_____

4. What does the ending paragraph in an article do?

_____

_____

5. Write a title for this opening paragraph that tells what the article will be about.

_____

Caucasoid people had light or dark skin, with either straight or curly hair, and came from the Caspian and Black Seas area. Mongoloid people came from Asia; they had flat faces and noses and dark skin. Negroid people came from Africa; their skin was dark, and they had curly hair and wide nostrils.

(Answers are on page 116.)

Articles

GETTING READY

You have read about what some prehistoric creatures' lives were like. In this part of the chapter, you will read about a group of Indians who still live very much like people did thousands of years ago. Dennis Werner, a scientist who studies people, went to live with a group of Amazon Indians to see what their lives were like.

Have you ever wanted to have an adventure in a faraway place? In 1976, Dennis Werner did just that. He traveled to the Amazon jungle in Brazil. There, among the Kayapo Indians, he had the adventure of a lifetime.

Amazon Adventure

Directions: Answer the questions after you read each part of this article.

Dennis Werner had many questions about the Kayapo Indians before he met them. He wondered what the Kayapo houses are like, what the Kayapo Indians eat, and how they spend their days. He also wondered what the Kayapo do for fun. By living with the Kayapo, Dennis Werner hoped to answer these and other questions.

Now that you have read the opening paragraph, think about the main idea of the article. Which sentence tells you what the article will be about? Go back and underline it.

One of the first things that Werner learned about was the Kayapo home. He discovered that the Kayapo live in mud houses with roofs made of woven palm leaves. The Kayapo build their houses in a double circle around a central place—an open-air meeting place. Werner himself lived in a Kayapo mud hut. It took some time for him to get used to it. He had to protect himself from snakes, rats, and bugs that would come into the hut during the night.

The first sentence of the paragraph above is the topic sentence. List three details that tell about the Kayapo homes.

a) _____

b) _____

c) _____

Werner also learned what the Kayapo eat and how they get their food. To get meat, the Kayapo men hunt monkeys and wild pigs. They also catch and eat fish. Werner joined the men on some of their long hunting trips. The Kayapo women have fruit and vegetable gardens. They grow sweet potatoes, bananas, pumpkins, and watermelons. Werner helped the women tend their gardens.

The topic sentence explains that Werner learned about Kayapo food and how they get it. List four details.

a) _____

b) _____

c) _____

d) _____

Werner discovered that the Kayapo enjoy games but do not like to compete against each other. They play a type of ball game in which they use sticks and fruit. But they do not keep score. In their culture, there is no such thing as winning or losing a game. They play to have fun and to try out their skills.

The topic sentence in the paragraph above tells you that the Kayapo like to play games but not to compete with each other. List three details that explain this.

a) _____

b) _____

c) _____

Werner lived with the Kayapo for about a year. The Kayapo had become as familiar to Werner as his friends at home. He answered many of his own questions about their lives, and he also came to love them as individuals. Werner later wrote a book about his experiences, called *Amazon Journey*.

How did Werner feel about the Kayapo after his year of living with them? List two details.

a) _____

_____

_____

b) _____

_____

_____

(Answers are on page 116.)

The ways in which people live and work have changed greatly during the past several thousand years. Can you imagine what life must have been like several thousand years ago?

Moving Away from the Stone Age

Directions: Answer the questions after you read each part of this article.

Throughout the past twelve thousand years, the way people have lived and worked has changed a lot as people's knowledge has grown. First, people were hunters and gatherers. Next, they learned how to farm and to settle in one place. And gradually, they lived in small towns and then larger cities.

What will this article be about? Find and write the main idea sentence.

_____

_____

_____

In the earliest times, men hunted large animals while the women and children gathered plants to eat. People had to move from place to place to find food. They learned how to make arrows and sharp-pointed spears so that they could hunt animals more easily.

What type of work did the earliest people do? Look for the topic sentence and write it on the lines.

_____

_____

_____

_____

Much later, people became farmers and settled in one place. They noticed that where seeds of grain were dropped, they grew. They also learned how to keep animals like wild sheep, goats, and cows. From these animals they could get meat, milk, and wool. Now that they did not have to move around, they built more permanent kinds of houses.

Gradually, people moved into small towns and villages and began trading and then buying and selling their goods. They learned how to measure and to count so that they could keep track of their belongings. As more and more people shared their ideas, even more important discoveries were possible.

Find and write the topic sentence of this paragraph. The paragraph tells the next type of work people did and how it changed their lives.

_____

_____

_____

_____

What are the last types of work mentioned in the article? Find and write the topic sentence on the lines.

_____

_____

_____

_____

(Answers are on page 116.)

USING WHAT YOU'VE LEARNED

Directions: The new skills that people of long ago learned affected the types of work they were able to do. Match the skills needed in each type of work. (One answer is used twice.)

_____ **1.** Using arrows and sharp-pointed spears   **a)** trading

_____ **2.** Mixing earth of different colors with water   **b)** hunting and gathering

_____ **3.** Keeping animals and growing grains   **c)** painting

_____ **4.** Making tools for cutting the grain   **d)** farming

_____ **5.** Exchanging goods that people made or grew

(Answers are on page 116.)

Thinking ABOUT Thinking

Part A

Facts can be proved true. They often contain names, dates, or exact numbers that can be checked.

Directions: Underline the part of each sentence that could make it a fact.

Example: The Amazon spreads over <u>3 million miles</u>.

1. Dennis Werner wrote his book about his experiences with the Kayapo Indians in 1984.

2. After one terrible war, only 60 percent of the Indians survived.

3. When Werner first came to live in the village, there were more than 285 new faces that he would have to learn to recognize.

4. In February of 1976, Werner boarded an airplane headed for the jungles of Brazil.

Part B

Opinions cannot be proved true or false. These sentences may contain words like *think, believe, feel, seems,* or *opinion*.

Directions: These sentences are opinions. Complete each sentence with one of the opinion words listed above.

Example: I *feel* it would be exciting to study and live with a group of people who are new to me.

1. Some people _____ that it is fascinating to study the bones and tools of people who lived thousands of years ago.

2. Many scientists _____ that there may be life in outer space.

3. It is my _____ that the U.S. government should spend more money on space exploration.

4. It _____ that people have lived in the universe for a longer time than we can imagine.

(Answers are on page 116.)

In this chapter, you learned that scientists have discovered a lot about how prehistoric creatures lived by studying fossilized skeletal bones, teeth, imprints on rocks, cave paintings, and so on. Now it is your turn to decide what clues you'd like to leave behind for people in future generations to discover about you.

Directions: Write a paragraph telling what things you would leave to be discovered. Then tell why you would leave them.

Future generations will be in for a big surprise when they discover what great things I have left for them to find. I will leave

_____

_____

_____

I will leave each of these things for a specific reason. These are my reasons:

_____

_____

_____

(Answers will vary.)

PASS IT ON

In this chapter, you learned some important information about how primitive people worked and lived. You learned about the ways of one group of Amazon Indians.

Pass on one new thing you learned in this chapter. By passing it on, you will remember the information better.

1. What new information that you learned in this chapter will you pass on?

_____

_____

2. Who will you pass it on to?

_____

(Answers will vary.)

4
Following Sequence

Being able to read directions and to follow sequence is a skill
you can use almost every day. Check (✔) which things you
have tried to make or put together.

- ☐ a special holiday meal
- ☐ a kite
- ☐ a cake
- ☐ a bookcase

To do these everyday activities, you need to be
able to follow directions. You have to read each step
very carefully, understand what it means, and do the steps in
the correct order.

In this chapter, you will learn how to read directions and
follow sequence. You will also learn about the importance of
time order when you read or write.

Tactics

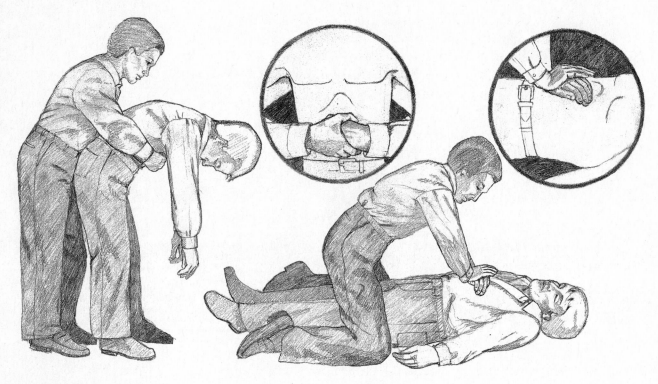

WARM-UP

Directions: First, use the pictures and the Part A directions to understand one form of the Heimlich maneuver. Then number the Part B directions in the correct order to understand a second form of the Heimlich maneuver.

Example: The Heimlich Maneuver

Part A: For a Choking Person Who Is Standing

_1_ Stand behind the choking person and wrap your arms around him.

_2_ Make a fist and place your thumb against the person's abdomen below the rib cage.

_3_ With your other hand, grasp your fist and, with a quick, upward movement, press your fists into the person's abdomen.

_4_ Repeat this motion several times until the food or object has been dislodged.

Part B: For a Choking Person Who Is Lying Down

_____ Repeat this motion several times until the food or object has been dislodged.

_____ Face the person who is lying on his back, and kneel down with his legs between your legs.

_____ Place your hands on top of each other, with the heel of your bottom hand resting against the person's abdomen below the rib cage.

_____ Using the heel of your bottom hand, make a quick, upward movement into the person's abdomen.

(Answers are on page 116.)

Following Directions

These four steps will help you read and follow directions.

1. Read all the directions completely and carefully to get a picture in your mind of what is to be done.

2. Go back and read just one step of the directions at a time.

3. Think about each step to see if you understand it.

4. Carry out the directions.

EXERCISE 1

Directions: Read these directions that tell how to make tacos. Then go back and number the steps in the correct order.

How to Make Tacos

_____ Fold up the finished tacos. Eat and enjoy.

_____ Gather what you need.

_____ Put small amounts of cooked hamburger, onions, tomatoes, lettuce, and shredded cheese in each cooked taco shell.

_____ Cut up onions, tomatoes, and lettuce. Fry crumbled hamburger; add taco mix and water. Cook until ready.

_____ Fry or microwave taco shells until they are hot.

(Answers are on page 116.)

MINDSTRETCHER

When you read directions, it is important to read all the steps first to completely understand the process. Then you can go back to each step, one by one.

Directions: Read each set of directions. Then answer the questions.

Direction Set A

- Step into the water.
- Keep your head and neck above the water.
- Paddle your arms and keep them moving for balance.
- Move your feet as if you were on a bicycle.

1. These directions teach you how to

   a) drown   **c)** tread water

   b) ride a bicycle   **d)** balance

2. What would happen if you didn't keep your legs and arms moving?

   _____

Direction Set B

- Slice a banana in half lengthwise and put it in a dish.
- Put three scoops of ice cream on top of the banana.
- Put your favorite topping and some nuts on the ice cream.
- Top it all off with whipped cream.

3. These directions teach you how to

   a) slice a banana   **c)** mix ice cream and nuts

   b) choose a topping   **d)** make a banana split

4. What would you be making if you didn't add the banana?

   _____

(Answers are on page 116.)

Sequence

Knowing the **sequence**, or the order, in which things happen, will help you understand and remember what you read. One type of sequence is called **time order**. History books, TV detective shows, and mystery books use time order. History books often use a **time line** to tell you the year when each important event happened.

EXERCISE 2

Directions: First, look at the time line. It shows the years when people bought these new inventions. Then <u>underline</u> the dates and inventions in the paragraph.

Time Line			
Year	**1940s**	**1950s**	**1980s**
Inventions	electric refrigerators	air conditioners televisions	VCRs computers

New Inventions

During the past 50 years, many inventions have changed the way people live. In the 1940s, electric refrigerators were introduced. Foods could now be kept fresh for longer periods of time. And people did not have to shop every day for fresh food.

In the 1950s, air conditioners and televisions became available. People could now keep their homes cool even during hot summer weather. Televisions introduced visual entertainment for the first time into people's everyday lives.

In the 1980s, people began to buy VCRs and computers. It became possible to record TV shows and watch them at a later time. Or people could rent movies and watch them at home instead of paying high prices to see films in theaters. Computers advanced the ways people could communicate with each other—in both their personal and professional lives. With computers came many exciting breakthroughs in medicine and science. We are indeed living in an age of important and exciting new discoveries and inventions.

(Answers are on page 116.)

Part A

Directions: First, read the directions for how to make french fries. Then put them into the correct order.

How to Make French Fries
- Put oil in a frying pan and heat the oil.
- Put the potatoes in the pan and fry them.
- Cut the potatoes into long, thin slices.
- Enjoy the french fries.
- Peel the skins from the potatoes.

1. _____

2. _____

3. _____

4. _____

5. _____

Part B

Directions: First, think of something you can make or do and write the steps in order. Then have someone else read the directions and see if he or she can follow them.

How to _____

1. _____

2. _____

3. _____

4. _____

5. _____

6. _____

(Answers are on page 117.)

EXERCISE 3

Directions: First, read this article about the Bermuda Triangle and look at the time line below. Then <u>underline</u> the important dates and events mentioned about the Bermuda Triangle.

Time Line				
Year	**1492**	**1872**	**1918**	**1973**
Event	Columbus's sailors reported glow in sea in that area	The *Mary Celeste* found floating with no one on it	Navy ship, the *Cyclops*, disappeared	Another ship, the *Anita*, disappeared

The Bermuda Triangle

Have you ever heard of the Bermuda Triangle? It is located in the part of the Atlantic Ocean that lies between Florida, Bermuda, and Puerto Rico. The shape of the area is roughly triangular, which explains how it got its name. The Bermuda Triangle is well known because of the many ships and airplanes that have disappeared there.

The mysteries of the Bermuda Triangle date back to the time of Christopher Columbus. In 1492, Columbus's sailors reported seeing a strange glow in the sea in that area. A large sailing ship, the *Mary Celeste*, was found floating in the area in 1872 with no one on board. Then, in 1918, a large navy ship, the *Cyclops*, disappeared. In more recent times, another large ship, the *Anita*, was reported missing in 1973.

More than 50 ships and 20 airplanes have mysteriously disappeared in the Bermuda Triangle. Some ships were found abandoned for no apparent reason. Other ships that sent out distress signals from there were never seen or heard from again. Not only were aircraft lost in the area but those who went to rescue the airplanes disappeared, too. To this day, no scientific explanation has been found to solve the mysteries of the Bermuda Triangle.

(Answers are on page 117.)

Time Order Signal Words

Writers often use signal words to show the time order in which things occurred. If they are telling the exact sequence of how something happened, as in a newspaper account, they might use words like *first, second,* and *third.*

Some other time order signal words include:

yesterday	**today**	**tomorrow**
before	**during**	**after**
first	**next**	**finally**
morning	**noon**	**night**

EXERCISE 4

Directions: Choose the correct time order signal word from the box. Write the word on the line before each sentence.

Example:

Yesterday, I went shopping for some new clothes.
Today, I am wearing my new red plaid shirt.
Tomorrow, I will wear my new brown leather coat.

1. _____ the game, we practiced every day.

_____ the game, we put in our best plays.

_____ the game, we were happy that we won.

2. _____, my alarm goes off loudly.

_____, I open my eyes wide in surprise.

_____, I get wearily out of bed.

3. In the _____, the sun rises in the east.

At _____, the sun shines directly overhead.

At _____, the sun sets in the west.

(Answers are on page 117.)

Directions: Imagine that you are on vacation. Write three things you will do. Write them in the order of importance to you.

First, _____

_____

Second, _____

_____

Third, _____

_____

(Answers will vary.)

CHECK-UP

Part A

Directions: First, read these directions. Then number the steps in correct order.

How to Remove a Splinter from Your Hand

_____ Sterilize a needle and tweezers with the flame from a match for a few seconds.

_____ Pull out the splinter; wash the area; put on a bandage.

_____ Press the cooled-off needle against the skin at the place of the splinter.

_____ Use tweezers to grasp the loosened end of the splinter.

_____ Push the splinter toward the place where it entered.

Part B

Directions: Complete each line using a time order signal word.

_____, I bought a turkey and some vegetables.

_____, I am cooking dinner for my family.

_____, we will be eating leftovers.

(Answers are on page 117.)

Articles

GETTING READY

You have learned how to read directions and to follow them step by step. You have also learned about the importance of time order and sequence when you read or write.

In this section, you will read about some famous people in history. You will be completing a time line as you read about each person's life. Filling in a time line about the important events in a person's life is a form of note taking. When you are studying for a test, you can read the time line to review the most important facts you learned.

Dr. Martin Luther King, Jr., is one of the most well-known leaders in modern American history. What do you know about his contributions? How have they affected your life?

Directions: Look at the time line about Dr. King's life. As you read the article about him, <u>underline</u> the dates that are given. Then fill in the missing events under each date.

		Time Line			
Year	1929	1953	1955	1964–1965	1968
Event	King is born.	King married Coretta Scott.	_____ _____ _____	_____ _____ _____	_____ _____ _____

Dr. Martin Luther King, Jr.

Personal Life

Martin Luther King, Jr., will be remembered in America for a long time as one of its most committed leaders. He was born in Georgia on January 15, 1929. His father was a minister, and King decided to become a Baptist preacher too. In 1953, he married Coretta Scott. They moved to Montgomery, Alabama and had four children.

Peaceful Demonstrations

In 1955, Dr. King organized a series of peaceful sit-ins and other demonstrations to show that black people should have the same rights as white people. He was inspired by the great leader of India, Mahatma Gandhi, who preached a message of nonviolent[1] protest.

Dr. King wanted black children to be able to attend the same schools as white children. He wanted black people to be able to eat in the same restaurants and use the same rest rooms as whites. He wanted black and white people to have equal voting and employment rights. Dr. King was thrown into jail again and again for leading peaceful marches to protest how unfairly black people were being treated in America.

What did Dr. King do in 1955 to help black people fight for their rights? Fill in this information on the time line.

Civil Rights and Voting Rights Acts

Finally, the Civil Rights Act of 1964 was passed. It authorized the federal government to desegregate[2] public places like schools, restaurants, and restrooms and open them up to all people, regardless of race. It also provided equal employment opportunities for all people. Because of his dream of peace and equal rights for all Americans, Dr. King was awarded the Nobel Peace Prize in 1964. One year later, the Voting Rights Act of 1965 was passed, so that all U.S. citizens who were eligible to vote could do so.

Which two important acts were passed by the federal government in 1964 and 1965? Which honor was Dr. King awarded in 1964? Write those on the time line.

---

[1] Standing up for rights in a peaceful way, without physical force.

[2] To stop the separation of races

A Tragic Ending

In the end, a tragic event occurred. On April 4, 1968, Dr. King, at age thirty-nine, was shot and killed on the balcony of a motel in Memphis, Tennessee. James Earl Ray was convicted of Dr. King's murder and sentenced to spend 99 years in jail. America lost a great man of peace and vision. The anniversary of Dr. King's birth is celebrated as a national holiday each year.

What tragic event happened in 1968? Write what happened on the time line on page 54.

Now answer these questions about the article.

1. What was happening in America that caused Dr. King to become a leader of his people?

   _____

   _____

   _____

   _____

2. Why do you think the U.S. government celebrates Martin Luther King, Jr. Day as a national holiday?

   _____

   _____

   _____

   _____

3. Do you think Martin Luther King, Jr. Day is an important holiday for black Americans or for all Americans? Why?

   _____

   _____

   _____

   _____

(Answers are on page 117.)

Jane Addams looked at the needs of young women from other countries who had just come to Chicago. She felt that, as a social worker, she could do much to help them. Do you know what social workers do?

Directions: As you read about Jane Addams's life, <u>underline</u> the dates. You will be writing what she did during each year listed on the time line.

Time Line	
Year	**Events**
1860	born
1883	_____
	_____
1889	_____
	_____
1909	_____
	_____
1910	_____
	_____
1915–1929	_____
	_____
1930	_____
	_____
1931	_____
	_____
1935	_____
	_____

Jane Addams

Hull House Opened

Jane Addams's life began in Cedarville, Illinois, in 1860. After years of study, she became a social worker in 1883 and visited a settlement house [3] in London. As a result of that trip she was inspired to open Hull House in Chicago, in 1889. Hull House was a neighborhood center for immigrants new to the city. It had a day-care center, a gymnasium, and a boardinghouse for young working women. Ms. Addams also offered the women college courses in art, music, and social work.

In Ms. Addams's time, many women had to work 10 to 12 hours a day. Her work with unions and other groups helped pass a law requiring a limit of eight working hours per day. Also, her work helped set up the first juvenile court, the first child labor law, and many housing reforms.

What important things did Ms. Addams do in 1883 and 1889? Fill in those events on the time line on page 57.

Leader for Women's Rights

Then, in 1909, Ms. Addams became the first president of the National Conference of Charities and Corrections—now called the National Conference on Social Welfare. Next, as president of the Women's International League for Peace and Freedom from 1915 to 1929, Ms. Addams led the fight for women's voting rights.

What did Ms. Addams do in 1909 and then from 1915 to 1929? Write those things on the time line on page 57.

Writings

Ms. Addams wrote several books. The best known were *Twenty Years at Hull House* (1910) and *The Second Twenty Years at Hull House* (1930). Ms. Addams was awarded the Nobel Peace Prize in 1931. She died on May 21, 1935, at age 75, leaving behind a legacy of change and reform for those in need.

What important things happened in Ms. Addams's life in 1910, 1930, 1931, and 1935? Write those events on the time line on page 57.

[3] A place that offers social services, educational, and recreational activities to people in an economically poor area

g the Farm Workers

. Chavez organized the grape
l established the National Farm
sociation. Next, in 1966, his
ged with another and was
United Farm Workers
: Committee. With this group,
ed a national boycott against
: growers because of the low
: were paid to the grape
nally, in 1970, the table grape
cepted the union and the
ded.

eir organization was renamed
Farm Workers (UFW). During
year, Mr. Chavez, with the
national boycott against
wers that lasted until 1978.

What did Mr. Chavez do in the
years 1962, 1966, 1970, and 1973?
Write that information on the time
line under each date on page 60.

At the present time, Mr. Chavez is
fighting for an end to pesticides [4] that are
sprayed on the crops and that are causing
the children of farm workers to get
cancer. He is still fighting for insurance
plans for the workers. He believes that
the most courageous act that men and
women can do is to spend their lives
struggling for justice in a nonviolent way.
His life is a testimony to that belief.

[4] Chemicals used for killing insects, weeds, etc.

r these questions about the article.

 there a need to organize farm workers into a

eople organize to claim their rights, there are risks
 s benefits. Have you ever been part of an
tion working for people's rights? Has anyone you
own?

t was the situation?

t was the risk?

t was the benefit?

(Answers are on page 117.)

Now answer these questions about the article.

1. What inspired Jane Addams to open Hull House?

_____

_____

2. Name four changes that Ms. Addams brought about
through her work with labor and other reform groups.

a) _____

b) _____

c) _____

d) _____

3. Is there a need for someone like Jane Addams in your
community today? What is one project that is greatly
needed in your neighborhood? Explain the project and
tell what you think could be done.

_____

_____

_____

_____

_____

_____

(Answers are on page 117.)

Cesar Chavez has spent his life as a spokesperson for farm workers' rights in the United States. Do you know what kind of work farm workers do? How are farm workers different from farmers?

Directions: As you read this article, <u>underline</u> the dates. Then fill in the missing information on the time line next to each date.

Time Line	
Year	**Event**
1927	born in Yuma, Arizona
1937	_____
1945	_____
1948	_____
1951	_____
1962	_____
1966	_____
1970	_____
1973	_____

Cesar Chavez

How the Farm

In 1951, Mr. Cha
organizer for the
Organization (C
Chavez learned
workers to fight
learned how to
He read everyth
educated as a le

At that time, far
than $1.20 an h
fruits or vegeta
the 3 million fa
were Filipinos,
Americans, and
were recruited
to work on the
migrant worke
days per year,
season.

The farm work
paid vacation,
overtime, and
benefits. They
for human life
enough to pay
and clothes fo

Cesar Chavez
workers need
that with a ur
for a decent r

Early Life

Cesar Chavez, a Mexican-American, was born in Yuma, Arizona, in 1927. His family owned a 160-acre farm, which they lost in 1937 when the bank would not renew their loan.

From then on, Cesar and his family became migrant farm workers. They were called migrants because they traveled from one part of the country to another, following the different crops as they became ripe for picking. They picked grapes and other fruits and vegetables on farms and so were called farm workers.

At 15, Cesar quit school to become a farm worker and to help support his family. He was drafted into the navy in 1945. In the spring of 1948, Mr. Chavez married his childhood sweetheart, Helen Fabela. They had three children, and they worked together as farm workers.

What important events happened in Mr. Chavez's life in 1937, 1945, and 1948? Write those events on the time line.

Which impo
Chavez mee
the direction
organization
this informa

Orga

In 196
picker
Worke
union
called
Organ
he org
table g
wages
pickers
grower
boycot

In 197:
the Un
that sa
UFW, le
lettuce

Now ans

1. Why
union

_____

2. When
as we
organ
have l

_____

a) Wl

_____

b) Wl

c) Wl

You have read about three people who have made a difference in other people's lives. Now you will have a chance to write about someone you know—someone who has made a difference.

Part A

Directions: Answer these questions.

1. Who is that person? _____

2. How do you know the person? _____

3. What has the person done to affect the lives of other people?

_____

_____

4. Have the person's actions been positive or negative?

_____

Part B

Directions: Now use the information you've given to write a paragraph about the person. Be sure to start with a topic sentence.

Example: Joe Hernandez has had a big impact on our neighborhood.

_____

_____

_____

_____

_____

_____

_____

_____

(Answers will vary.)

Thinking ABOUT Thinking

As you read, it is important to know the difference between facts and opinions. **Facts** often contain dates and can be proved.

Example: Jane Addams wrote *Twenty Years at Hull House* in 1910.

Opinions state beliefs. They may contain words like *best, most, all, greatest,* and *any.*

Example: Cesar Chavez is the <u>greatest</u> organizer of his time.

Directions: Write **F** if the statement is a fact. Write **O** if the statement is an opinion.

_____ **1.** Martin Luther King, Jr., was born in Georgia in 1929.

_____ **2.** All people should try to make the world safer.

_____ **3.** The greatest people are world leaders.

_____ **4.** Jane Addams received the Nobel Peace Prize in 1931.

_____ **5.** The Civil Rights Act was passed in 1964.

_____ **6.** Chavez was more organized than any other union leader.

_____ **7.** Jane Addams was the most important reformer of her time.

_____ **8.** Cesar Chavez organized the grape pickers in 1962.

_____ **9.** About 70% of Mexican-Americans live in California.

_____ **10.** Dr. King was the best leader for the civil rights movement.

_____ **11.** *Twenty Years at Hull House* was written by Jane Addams in 1910.

_____ **12.** I think all people believe in the need for world peace.

_____ **13.** Cesar Chavez was a migrant farm worker himself.

(Answers are on page 118.)

USING WHAT YOU'VE LEARNED

Directions: There are always reasons why people become involved in fighting for people's rights. Match each person's action with the reason why he or she became involved.

_____ **1.** Martin Luther King, Jr., organized peaceful sit-ins and demonstrations.

a) Women immigrants needed day care for their children while they worked and studied.

_____ **2.** Jane Addams founded Hull House in Chicago.

b) Black Americans did not have equal rights.

_____ **3.** Cesar Chavez organized boycotts against table grape and lettuce growers.

c) Migrant workers had no unions to protect them.

(Answers are on page 118.)

PASS IT ON

You have learned some information about three famous Americans who fought for people's rights. When you pass on information, you do yourself a favor, because you learn and remember the information better.

1. What new information that you learned in this chapter will you pass on?

_____

_____

_____

_____

2. Who will you pass it on to?

_____

(Answers will vary.)

5
Comparison and Contrast

Have you ever had trouble deciding what brand to buy at the grocery store? If you are like most people, you have to consider many things.

When buying lunch meat, you may face a choice like this:

ALL STAR HAM $1.99 per lb. 100 calories per slice 300 milligrams of sodium per slice 6% fat per slice imported	**BEST BUY HAM** $1.79 per lb. 150 calories per slice 280 milligrams of sodium per slice 8% fat per slice domestic (American)

Which ham would you buy? _____

Why? _____

To make a choice, check (✔) what things you considered.

☐ price   ☐ sodium
☐ calories   ☐ imported or domestic
☐ fat

In this chapter, you will use what you know about comparing things to look at how things are alike or different. This is what writers do when they compare and contrast things.

Tactics

| 1985 Sunset TMX. 125,000 mi. 25 m.p.g. Engine needs work. Asking $3,000 | 1990 Sunset TMX. 25,000 mi. 20 m.p.g. Engine needs work. Asking $6,000 |

WARM-UP

Directions: Look at these two want ads. Tell whether each set of facts about the two cars is the *same* or *different.*

Example: number of miles ___different___

1. condition of engine

_____

2. year of car

_____

3. model of car

_____

4. cost

_____

5. miles per gallon

_____

6. Which items are the same?

_____

7. Which items are different?

_____

_____

(Answers are on page 118.)

Same and Different

When you looked at the ads for the cars, you looked for the things that were the *same* and the things that were *different*. When writers show things that are the *same*, they **compare**. When writers show things that are *different*, they **contrast**.

EXERCISE 1

Part A

Directions: Read each set of sentences. If they describe two things that are the same, write **same**. If they describe two things that are different, write **different**.
Note: These sentences compare *industrialized* countries with *developing* countries. What do you think these words mean?

_____

_____

Industrialized countries, like the United States, already have many factories and services for the people. Developing countries, such as China, are still building their factories and their services.

_____ **1.** Most industrialized countries are in Europe and North America. On the other hand, most developing countries are in South America, Africa, and Asia.

_____ **2.** People in industrialized countries live to be an average of 71 years old. However, people in developing countries live to be an average of 63 years old.

_____ **3.** Industrialized countries must get rid of their garbage. Developing countries must also get rid of their waste materials.

_____ **4.** Like industrialized countries, developing countries are concerned about the health of their citizens.

_____ **5.** Most people in industrialized countries have indoor plumbing. But in developing countries, many people use outdoor toilets and use rainwater for washing.

Part B

Now use what you have learned to write two paragraphs. Tell how developing and industrialized countries are the same and how they are different. Write your paragraphs on another piece of paper.

(Answers are on page 118.)

Directions: Think about how each pair of words is the **same**. Then think how each pair of things is **different**. Write your ideas in each box.

Things	pen	pencil
Same		
Different		
Things	house	apartment
Same		
Different		
Things	speech	sales talk
Same		
Different		

(Answers will vary.)

Signal Words

Certain signal words and phrases are used when things are compared to show how they are **alike**:

like	**similarly**	**the same as**
similar	**alike**	**both**
also	**as**	

Other signal words and phrases are used when things are contrasted to show how they are **different**:

differences	**on the other hand**	**but**
other	**compared with**	**unlike**
different from	**compared to**	**however**
while	**more**	**less**

EXERCISE 2

Directions: In the following paragraphs, schools in Europe and the United States are being compared and contrasted. Find and <u>underline</u> the signal words that show how they are alike or different.

There are many <u>differences</u> between the schools in Europe and the schools in the United States. In Europe, students go to school more days of the year. Also, students in Europe get more homework than in the United States. European students take school more seriously because they must take tests to stay in school.

People in both countries are concerned with how well their children are learning. Compared with sixteen other industrialized countries, the United States was fifteenth in the amount of money spent on high schools and grade schools. Compared with the other industrialized countries, American students do poorly in math and science. For these reasons, American teachers and parents are putting more effort into the education of their children.

(Answers are on page 118.)

EXERCISE 3

Part A

Directions: Read the following paragraph. It tells some ways in which the United States and Sweden are **alike**. The two countries are being compared. Write the correct signal word from the box on each blank line.

also	alike	both	like

In many ways, the United States and Sweden are

_____. In _____ countries, people vote for

their leaders. The United States, _____ Sweden, has

many industries. _____, both Sweden and the United

States are rich countries.

Part B

Directions: Read the following paragraph. It tells some ways in which Sweden and the United States are **different**. The two countries are being contrasted. Write the correct signal word or phrase from the box on each blank line.

on the other hand	but	however

In many ways, Sweden and the United States are different.

Sweden spends 48 percent of its national budget on social

services. _____, the United States spends only a small

percent of its budget on social services. In Sweden, almost all

medical care is free, _____ the United States provides

little free medical care. In Sweden, everyone over 67 years of

age receives money from the government. _____, in

the United States, only older people who have worked and

their spouses receive social security.

(Answers are on page 118.)

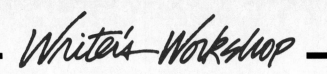
Writer's Workshop

Directions: Answer these questions in your own words.

1. Write two things that are the same about American and European schools.

   _____

   _____

2. Write two things that are different about American and European schools.

   _____

   _____

3. Tell one thing that could be done to make American schools better. Give a reason why you think this would work.

   _____

   _____

   _____

   (Answers will vary.)

CHECK-UP

Directions: Write your answers on the blank lines. Look back at the chapter if you do not know an answer.

1. When you compare and contrast things, you look for how

   things are the _____ and how they are

   _____.

2. Write two signal words or phrases that are used to

   compare things. _____   _____

3. Write two signal words or phrases that are used to contrast

   things. _____   _____

(Answers are on page 118.)

Articles

GETTING READY

Now that you have learned how to look for how things are alike or different, you are ready to use these skills. In this section, you will read articles about common problems facing the United States and some other countries. You will learn how to **compare** and **contrast** their approaches to these problems.

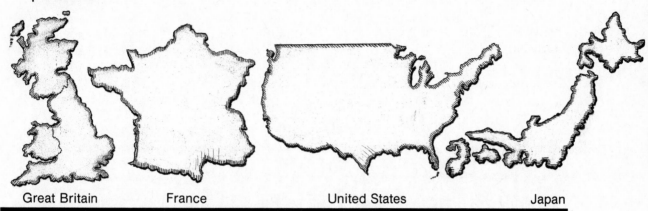

Great Britain   France   United States   Japan

> Do you have a friend, coworker, or relative living in another country? If so, you know that every country faces the same problems, but the solutions are often different. How does the United States handle day care, health insurance, and recycling, as compared to other countries?

Common Problems

Directions: As you read the article, underline the signal words that show comparison and contrast about each problem. Then answer the questions. When you finish, you will have a list of notes about important facts you learned.

Day Care

Both American and French parents must send their preschool-age children to day-care centers while they work each day. In both countries, day-care centers are staffed by trained teachers. However, unlike the U.S. government, the French government pays for additional training for its teachers.

1. List one way in which the U.S. and French day-care systems are alike.

_____

_____

_____

The French government provides six hours of free day care every day for all three- to five-year-old children. French parents have to pay only $210 per year if they need more than six hours of day care each day for their children. On the other hand, American parents often pay $200–$400 per month for day-care services for their children. While the U.S. government gives a small tax break to help parents pay for day care, it pays for day care only for children of low-income families.

2. List two ways in which the U.S. and French governments are different in their support for day care.

a) _____

b) _____

3. Why do you think that the U.S. government pays for day care for children from low-income families?

_____

_____

Have you ever had a medical problem that required a doctor's care or that required you to stay in a hospital? Paying for this care is a major concern for anyone who needs medical care.

Medical Care

Medical care is an important issue in both the United States and Great Britain. About 15 percent of U.S. citizens do not have any health insurance at all. But in Great Britain, the government provides free health care for all of its citizens. In the United States, some employees have to pay for part of their insurance costs out of their paychecks each month. On the other hand, taxes pay for all medical expenses for persons in Great Britain.

In the United States, people do not have to wait very long to see a doctor or to have surgery. However, people in Great Britain often have to wait several months

4. Contrast the costs of medical care in the United States and Great Britain.

_____

_____

5. What could the United States learn from Great Britain about funding medical care?

_____

_____

6. Contrast the waiting time for medical care in each country.

_____

_____

to see a doctor or to have surgery. In both countries, the quality of medical care varies widely. In the United States, people with good incomes and insurance tend to get better medical care than those who are poor and have no insurance. But in Great Britain, younger people seem to receive faster medical treatment than older adults.

7. What factors seem to make a difference in the quality of medical care given to people in the United States and in Great Britain?

_____

_____

_____

Is recycling being done in your neighborhood? How to dispose of waste is a problem facing countries all over the world today.

Recycling Garbage

The United States and Japan both face the problem of recycling, or disposing of, their garbage. While the United States recycles only 7 percent of its paper and glass, Japan recycles 50 percent of its paper and glass.

Landfills, where garbage is stored, are another source of concern. Most U.S. landfills are not protected against leakage. The land and water around landfills can be poisoned if leakage occurs. But in Japan, landfills are protected against leakage. Efforts have been made in both countries to improve the methods for recycling garbage. In Japan, the government has taken a strong stand about recycling. And in the United States, after Earth Day 1990, citizens became much more aware and actively involved in recycling their garbage.

8. Contrast the amount of recycling of paper and glass done by the United States and Japan.

_____

_____

9. What can happen if landfills are not protected from leakage?

_____

_____

10. What event helped people in the United States become more aware of the need for recycling their garbage?

_____

_____

11. How can the United States handle its problem of recycling garbage in a better way? What things would you suggest?

_____

_____

(Answers are on page 119.)

USING WHAT YOU'VE LEARNED

Directions: Countries often try to solve problems by using the four steps below. Match each step with the reason why the step is important. The first one has been done for you.

Steps

___d___ **1.** Local people got involved.

_____ **2.** The national government got involved.

_____ **3.** The problem was looked at very closely to see what was needed.

_____ **4.** Plans were made to solve the problem in a complete and daring way.

Reason why step is important

a) To solve a problem, you must think about it carefully.

b) The national government can see how a problem touches all parts of the country and can find the money and the experts to solve the problem.

c) Big problems must be solved with complete and daring solutions.

d) Local people should be involved since they are the ones who have the problem and need to find a solution.

(Answers are on page 119.)

Have you ever visited Japan? Do you know how Japanese family life, work, and school systems compare to ours? This interview is with Bob Harris, an American businessman who lived in Japan for five years.

Interview with Bob Harris about Japan

Directions: Answer the questions after you read this article.

Q: How are Americans and Japanese the same?

A: People are the same everywhere. Wherever you go, you will find kind people, selfish people, honest people, and dishonest people.

Q: What would you say is the biggest difference between the Japanese and the Americans?

A: Many Japanese ways are different from American ways. Most Japanese people are very polite. It is hard to know when a Japanese person is angry or upset. Sometimes Japanese people will say yes even when they mean no. In Japanese culture, this is not lying. It is just part of being polite.

There are other differences, too. I am an American. I have a family, and I work for a company. But I don't usually think of myself as an American or as one part of a family or a company. I just think of myself as me, Bob Harris. The Japanese always think of themselves as part of a bigger group.

1. How are Americans and Japanese people the same?

_____

_____

2. Japanese people are "polite" in ways that Americans are not. Explain the difference.

_____

_____

_____

3. Name one difference between the ways Americans and Japanese people think of themselves.

_____

_____

_____

Q: What is work like in Japan?
A: Many workers think of their companies as a big family. These workers believe that if they do not do their best, they will hurt the rest of the family—the other workers. Most factory workers work six days a week. Japanese businessmen spend their evenings taking clients to dinner.

There is a lot of competition among Japanese factories. I believe this attitude helps workers in Japanese factories make good products.

Q: What is education like in Japan?
A: To get a good job in Japan, you must have a good education. In Japan, a good education means going to a good school. Children take tests at different ages to see which schools they can go to. These tests are very important. After school each day, many students go to special tutors who will help them pass the tests.

Q: Please describe Japanese family life.
A: Family life is very important to the Japanese people. The Japanese mother is the heart of the family. Most Japanese mothers do not work outside the home. They devote themselves to their children. Japanese mothers help their children with homework and take the children to special tutors.

Japanese fathers do not spend much time with their families because they work long hours and on Saturdays. But Japanese fathers are obeyed. When the Japanese father says something, everyone listens.

4. How do Japanese people view the companies they work for?

_____

_____

_____

_____

5. Do you think competition is a good motivator for factory workers? Why or why not?

_____

_____

_____

_____

6. Why are tests so important in the Japanese school system?

_____

_____

_____

_____

7. Name three facts you learned about Japanese family life.

a) _____

_____

b) _____

_____

c) _____

_____

Q: Does Japan have any problems?

A: Japan has many problems. One of Japan's biggest problems is lack of space. Apartment houses are crowded together. People live in small apartments, and rents are very high. In the cities, there are not enough parks or open spaces.

There is also a problem with social services. Most companies do not have pension plans. People feel pushed to work hard and save because they are afraid of having no money in old age.

8. Name two problems Japanese people face in the cities.

_____

_____

_____

_____

_____

(Answers are on page 119.)

Writer's Workshop

Directions: Now it is your turn to describe something about the United States to someone from another country. Read the sample topic, details, and paragraph.

Topic: What Bothers Some Americans about Their Work
Detail A: not interesting or challenging enough
Detail B: feel they are underpaid
Detail C: do not have enough vacation time

What Bothers Some Americans about Their Work
There are three things that bother some Americans about their work. First, they wish their jobs were more interesting and challenging. Second, they would like to receive more pay for the work they do. Finally, they would like to have more vacation time to travel or to spend time with their families or friends. If these changes were made, Americans would feel better about their work.

Fill in the details of the following topic. Then write your paragraph on another piece of paper.

Topic: What I Like Best or Least about School

Detail A: _____

Detail B: _____

Detail C: _____

(Answers will vary.)

Part A

Directions: The following sentence contains a fact. Change the fact to an opinion. First, read the opinion words below the sentence. Then add an opinion word to the sentence. Finally, tell why you chose that opinion word to describe Japan.

Example: Japan is a country.
    Opinion words: beautiful   competitive   wonderful
    Japan is a <u>beautiful</u> country.
    Reason: I think Japan is a beautiful country because it is made up of four small islands and several mountains.

The Japanese are a people.

Opinion words: polite   hardworking   nonviolent

The Japanese are a _____ people.

Reason: _____

_____

Part B

Directions: Read the following opinion and the two facts that support that opinion. Then write an opinion of your own about Japan and two facts to support it.

Example: **Opinion:** Japan has a very strict educational system.
    Fact: Children must take tests to see which schools they can go to.
    Fact: Children go to tutors who will help them pass the tests.

Opinion: _____

Fact: _____

Fact: _____

(Answers will vary.)

USING WHAT YOU'VE LEARNED

Directions: Read these descriptions about life in Japan. Put a **yes** next to the things that you could live with. Put a **no** next to the things you would not like to live with.

_____ almost no violent crime

_____ almost everyone finishes high school

_____ most mothers do not work outside the home

_____ children take tests to see which schools they can go to

_____ most people work six days a week

_____ without pension plans, older people fear running out of money when they can no longer work

_____ small apartments cost a lot to rent

_____ cities have few parks or open spaces

(Answers will vary.)

PASS IT ON

You have learned some important information about different countries. You know how some other countries have solved their problems. You know how the United States has tried to solve the same problems. You know some ways that the people of the United States and Japan are alike and different.

When you pass on information, you do someone else a favor. You also do yourself a favor. When you explain information to someone else, it helps you understand and remember it better.

1. What new information that you've learned in this chapter will you pass on?

   _____

   _____

   _____

   _____

2. Who will you pass this information on to?

   _____

(Answers will vary.)

6

Cause and Effect

Have you learned how to do something new lately? What was it? How did it make you feel? Check (✔) the statements that happened to you as a result.

- ☐ **I learned new information.**
- ☐ **I felt better about my future.**
- ☐ **I felt more confident.**

Write one other thing that happened as a result.

_____

In a cause-and-effect sentence, one thing happens. Then, as a result, another thing happens.

Example: | cause | Because I learned how to read a map,

| effect | I can go places without getting lost.

You know from your own life that, if one thing happens, another thing can result. The first thing that happens is the **cause**. The thing that happens as a result is the **effect**.

In this chapter, you will see how writers use this cause-and-effect relationship when they write sentences and paragraphs.

Tactics

cause

effect

WARM-UP

Directions: Each of the following sentences has a cause and an effect. Look for the thing that happens first. <u>Underline</u> the **cause**. Then look for what happens as a result. Circle the **effect**.

Example: <u>Steve watched his diet,</u> (so he began to lose weight.)

1. Since the movie was very funny, Gina laughed a lot.

2. The woman had a car accident; as a result, her insurance rates went up.

3. After the man heard that his wife had triplets, he fainted.

4. Eva watered the plant every day; consequently, the plant grew large green leaves.

5. Because the music on the radio was playing so loudly, I didn't hear the doorbell ring.

(Answers are on page 119.)

Cause and Effect in Sentences

As you saw in the warm-up exercise, first one thing happened (the cause). Then another thing happened as an outcome of the first action or event (the effect).

Now you will see that the cause or the effect can be written first or last in a sentence. No matter which is written first, the cause or the effect, the relationship stays the same.

EXERCISE 1

Directions: Read each pair of sentences. Notice that each pair of sentences has the same cause-and-effect relationship, regardless of the order in which it is written. Write *cause* or *effect* on each line.

Example: cause Luis returned the lost wallet to its owner,

effect so the owner gave Luis a reward.

effect The owner gave Luis a reward

cause because Luis returned the wallet to its owner.

_____ **1.** The car broke down,

_____ so the driver took the car to be repaired.

_____ The driver took the car to be repaired

_____ after the car broke down.

_____ **2.** Margo won the lottery,

_____ so she bought a new house.

_____ Margo bought a new house

_____ after she won the lottery.

_____ **3.** Because Jane stepped on a piece of glass,

_____ she went to the emergency room.

_____ Jane went to the emergency room

_____ because she stepped on a piece of glass.

(Answers are on page 119.)

EXERCISE 2

Directions: Read these sentences. Some sentences tell the **cause**. Other sentences tell the **effect**. Choose the correct cause or effect sentence from the box. Write the sentence on the line where it fits best.

Possible causes and effects:
- The land has good soil.
- People get less exercise, and they read less.
- Kids can play computer games, and adults can write letters and keep track of their bills.
- People receive improved medical care today.

---

1. (effect) Many people live longer today.

(cause) _____

2. (cause) Many families have computers in their homes.

(effects) _____

_____

3. (effect) Farmers in the United States can feed thousands of people.

(cause) _____

4. (cause) Watching too much television can have bad results.

(effects) _____

_____

(Answers are on page 119.)

In this Writer's Workshop, you will be completing each sentence by making up an effect, or a thing that could happen as a result of the first action.

Part A
Directions: Think of one thing that could happen as an outcome of the first action in each sentence. Write an *effect* on each line.

1. Our teacher was not in school tonight, so

_____

2. When Tom got stung by a bee,

_____

3. Since my friend bought me a birthday gift,

_____

4. Because I forgot to hand in my paper,

_____

5. Due to the fact that the plane was delayed for three hours,

_____

Part B
Directions: What do you think are the three most important effects of getting a good education? Complete each sentence with your own ideas. When you have finished, you will have completed a cause-and-effect paragraph. Reread your paragraph to make sure it clearly states your ideas.

There are many important effects of getting a good education. One

important effect is that _____

A second important effect is that _____

_____

A third important effect is that _____

_____

(Answers will vary.)

MINDSTRETCHER

Directions: Read the following questions. Write your own ideas on the blank lines.

1. What are four causes of being late for school or work?

   a) _____

   b) _____

   c) _____

   d) _____

2. What are four effects of being late for school or work?

   a) _____

   b) _____

   c) _____

   d) _____

3. **a)** Is there something you are always late for? What is it?

   _____

   b) What is the cause of your being late?

   _____

   c) What is the effect of your being late?

   _____

4. <u>Underline</u> only the sentences that have a true cause-and-effect relationship. Don't be fooled by superstition!

   a) After Tom walked under a ladder, he broke his arm.

   b) After Tom tripped on a curb, he broke his arm.

   c) Because a black cat crossed Kim's path, she was hit by a car.

   (Answers are on page 119.)

Signal Words

When you read the sentences in the warm-up exercise, you identified a *cause* and an *effect* in each sentence. But did you know that each sentence contained a **signal word** or **phrase**? Writers sometimes use certain signal words and phrases to help you identify the cause or the effect in their sentences and paragraphs.

Signal words that show *cause* and *effect* include:

because	**therefore**	**reasons why**
so/so that	**effect**	**consequently**
as a result	**causes**	**since**
due to	**follows**	**if . . . then**

EXERCISE 3

Part A

Directions: Read this paragraph. It tells causes or reasons why women are waiting until they are older to have children. Underline the correct signal word or phrase in each sentence. Then write the *causes* on the blank lines below the paragraph.

There are many reasons why young women are waiting to have children. Some women wait because they want to get an education before they have children. Others wait so that they can get their careers started first. Some women wait to save money before they have children. And finally, many women are waiting due to medical advances that have made it safer for older women to have children.

The paragraph gives four reasons why some women are waiting until they are older to have children. What are the reasons?

a) _____

b) _____

c) _____

d) _____

Part B

Directions: Read this paragraph. It tells two effects, or things that have happened, as a result of money and effort spent on space exploration. <u>Underline</u> the signal words. Look for the *effects* as you read this paragraph.

There are at least two reasons why spending money and effort on space exploration has been helpful to people on Earth. Solving the problems of space travel and communication has led to two important inventions. First, because of the space program, we now have very powerful monitors used in hospitals. The monitors were developed so that the men orbiting in space could talk with those in charge of the space flight down on Earth. Second, as a result of money spent on the space program, microchips were developed for the computers used in space rockets. Microchips are now used in personal computers on Earth.

Two effects of money and effort spent on space exploration are:

a) _____

b) _____

(Answers are on page 119.)

CHECK-UP

Directions: Write your answers to the questions on the blank lines. Look back through the chapter if you do not know an answer.

1. The reason why something happens is called

the _____.

The thing that happens as a result is called

the _____.

2. Write four signal words or phrases that show a cause-and-

effect relationship. _____ _____

_____ _____

(Answers are on page 119.)

Articles

Now that you have learned about **cause-and-effect** relationships in sentences and in paragraphs, you are ready to see how these relationships are used in the articles you will read.

In this section, you will read about why some U.S. factories are closing, why a father wants his son to stay in school, and how to be ready for service jobs in the future.

Many U.S. factories have closed in the past 20 years. Why do you think this has been happening? How many American-made products do you own? Do you think this makes a difference?

Fewer Factory Jobs

Directions: Take notes as you read this article. When you finish, you will have a list of important facts you learned from this article.

In many ways, American people are well off. Almost 100 percent of U.S. households have electricity. Ninety-nine percent of the households have radios. Ninety-eight percent have televisions. Ninety-two percent have at least one telephone. Eighty-seven percent have at least one car. And 73 percent have washing machines.

Even though Americans have many things, many people cannot find well-paying jobs. In the past, some people found high-paying jobs in factories. But in the past twenty years, factories all over the United States have closed. Thousands of factory workers have lost their jobs. In the 1990s, even more factories may close or cut back their work force.

What is one reason that many U.S. factories are closing? Look at the label on your shirt, sweater, or jacket. Where was it made?

In many cases, your clothing was not made in the United States. Why? The owners of many companies have put their factories in countries such as Taiwan and Korea. They do that because they can pay factory workers in Taiwan and Korea as little as $5 a week!

Two major industries that have laid off workers are the automobile industry and the industries that make electronic appliances. In 1953, the United States produced 80 percent of the world's automobiles and 90 percent of the world's television sets. Today, the United States produces fewer than 30 percent of the world's automobiles and televisions.

Many people buy VCRs, televisions, and cars made in other countries. Most of these people believe that those products have better quality for lower prices. Many people think that there are two main reasons why other countries make better products.

First, some people say that the United States does not have the engineers or scientists needed to develop new products. These people believe that the United States should spend more money on education—especially on science and math education.

Second, other people say that U.S. workers are not as involved in their work as are workers in other countries. In some countries, workers get rewards or bonuses that are based on the amount of

1. Are most Americans better off now than they were 100 years ago? Explain.

_____

_____

_____

_____

2. Why are some U.S. factories closing today? List two causes.

a) _____

b) _____

3. Why do some Americans prefer to buy products made in other countries?

_____

_____

4. Which two areas of education could help the United States make better products?

a) _____

b) _____

5. What two effects can result when workers get rewards and bonuses from their company?

a) _____

b) _____

money made by their companies. These workers go out of their way to learn new skills. Their companies also encourage them to make suggestions to improve their factory's products.

Now you know some reasons why many factories in the United States have closed. While many factories are still open, some workers are being replaced by machines. Many of these machines do the work of ten or more people! As a result, even more workers are losing their factory jobs. Factory owners say that they need these machines to compete with other companies.

6. Do you think that workers should be replaced by machines? Why or why not?

_____

_____

(Answers are on page 120.)

Writer's Workshop

In this Writer's Workshop, you will be asked to write a letter giving advice about getting a good job.

Directions: Write a letter to your child or to a friend about getting a good job. What ideas will you include? Make a list of ideas and then write those ideas in the form of a letter. You may want to use the letter from the father to his son on the next page as a model.

Dear _____,

_____

_____

_____

_____

_____

_____

(Answers will vary.)

As you read the following letter from a father to his son, think about how staying in school can have a positive effect on a person's work life. Why have you decided to continue your education?

Father to Son

Directions: Answer the questions after you read this letter.

Dear Jack,

When I was your age, I went to work in a factory. I never really got good at reading and writing. But it didn't seem to matter.

Ten years ago, my boss asked me to be a foreman. But I knew I couldn't read or write well enough to do all the paperwork. I turned down the job. That's when your mother went back to work.

Even today on the job, I can't read all the instructions for operating the new machines. I'm afraid of two things—that I might break a machine or I might cause someone to get hurt. Would you want to live with that fear?

I don't want you to have the same problems I do. You think it would be better to quit school and look for a job. But, as your father, I'm asking you to learn from my mistakes.

Stay in school and learn as much as you can. Your mother and I only want the best for you, Son. Your mother had to help me write this letter. Let me know if you have read this, Jack.

Love,
Dad

1. What caused the father to turn down the job as a foreman?

   _____

   _____

2. What is the father afraid might happen on his job?

   a) _____

   b) _____

3. What effect do you think this letter may have on Jack? Why?

   _____

   _____

(Answers are on page 120.)

A Service Job in Your Future?

Directions: Read this article. Then answer the questions.

During the next ten years, there won't be many job openings for factory workers. But there will be many job openings for service workers. Who are "service workers"? While factory workers make a product, service workers provide a service to others. Doctors, teachers, dry cleaners, salespersons, and clerks are all service workers.

As we enter the next century, there will be many jobs for service workers. But there will also be a major problem. Many service workers will not be well paid—especially service workers who do not have a skill or special training. For example, fast-food workers do not make a lot of money.

To make sure that you get a well-paying service job, you need to follow three steps. First, find out what jobs will be in demand. For example, experts predict that the demand for medical and computer workers will be high. Second, select a job that meets your needs, interests, and abilities. Third, find and get training for the job you want.

1. What is the difference between the work done by factory workers and service workers?

_____

_____

_____

_____

2. Name one problem that service workers face.

_____

_____

3. What three steps should you take to get a well-paying service job?

a) _____

b) _____

c) _____

To find a well-paying service job, you also need to find someone who can help you with these three steps. The person should know about the future of the job market, help you look at your needs and interests, and know where you can find training.

It may take some work to find this person. It could be a friend or a job counselor. But once you get the job you want, your effort will be worth it.

4. What three things can a good job counselor help you discover?

a) _____

b) _____

c) _____

5. Why do you think it is important to find a job that meets your needs, interests, and abilities?

_____

_____

(Answers are on page 120.)

USING WHAT YOU'VE LEARNED

Another important part of finding a good job is to know how to handle the interview process. If you do well in an interview, you have a better chance of getting a job.

Part A

Directions: Put a check (✔) next to the things you have found helpful in interviewing for a job.

- ☐ having a friendly attitude
- ☐ answering questions honestly
- ☐ finding out information about the company
- ☐ knowing what training or skills are needed for the job
- ☐ knowing what educational level is expected
- ☐ identifying your interests and abilities related to the job
- ☐ knowing the names and addresses of friends, coworkers, and former employers who can recommend you for the job

Part B

Directions: To help you prepare for getting a job, fill out this information about yourself.

1. *Job Objective* (job you want to do)

_____

_____

2. *Work Experience*

_____

_____

3. *Education/Training*

_____

_____

4. *Your Skills for the Job*

_____

_____

_____

5. *Interests Related to the Job*

_____

_____

_____

6. *References* (people who can recommend you)

_____

_____

_____

(Answers will vary.)

Thinking ABOUT Thinking

Directions: Each opinion is followed by two reasons. Decide which reason gives better support for the opinion and put a check (✔) by that sentence.

Example: Opinion: There is life in outer space.

☐ **Reason a:** The space creatures in movies look so real that they must be based on real space creatures.
☐ **Reason b:** The materials needed to support life can be found in space.

1. **Opinion:** Thomas Edison was a great American inventor.
   ☐ **Reason a:** Thomas Edison invented more than a thousand items.
   ☐ **Reason b:** Thomas Edison lived from 1847 to 1931.
2. **Opinion:** The computer is one of the most important inventions.
   ☐ **Reason a:** Many people play computer games.
   ☐ **Reason b:** Computers have changed the way that people work and communicate.

(Answers are on page 120.)

PASS IT ON

You have learned some important information in this chapter. You know how quickly life has changed in recent years. You know why some U.S. factories have closed. You know three steps that will help you find a good-paying service job.

Remember that information is important in today's world. With information, you can help change the world. You can change yourself. Information is to be prized and shared.

1. What new information that you learned in this chapter will you pass on?

   _____

2. Who will you pass it on to?

   _____

(Answers will vary.)

7
Outlining and Summarizing

Imagine that you and a friend are thinking about getting away for a weekend. To plan for this getaway, fill in the following ideas:

Getaway Weekend

- **Where you will go**

  _____

- **What you will do**

  _____

  _____

- **What you will need to take**

  _____

  _____

In writing down your ideas in this form, you have created an **outline**. Writers often make an outline before they begin to write. After you read, one way to study is to outline the most important ideas in the article or chapter.

Knowing how to **summarize** what you have read is also important. When you summarize, you remember the main ideas and write them in sentences in your own words. In this chapter, you will learn how to summarize. You will also learn about the future.

Tactics

WARM-UP

Directions: Look at this sample outline. It tells where some homes and cities may be built in the future, as we run out of space or need to be protected from air pollution. Fill in your own ideas on the last three lines.

Sample Outline: Future Homes and Cities

I. Where future homes may be built
   A. in domes under the sea
   B. under the ground away from air pollution
   C. on barges in the sea
II. Where future cities may be built
   A. in gigantic enclosed buildings
   B. under a large dome or protective shell
   C. in space stations on other planets
III. Why we may need different places to build homes

   A. _____

   B. _____

   C. _____

(Answers will vary.)

Why Make an Outline?

Making an outline is a quick and useful way to organize the information you read about a topic. It helps you focus on the main ideas and supporting details. After you have read the passage and made the outline, you can read the outline again to review the passage.

How do you outline a passage? First, read it over once, paying attention to the main ideas and details. Then read the passage again. Write down the two or three main ideas you want to write about. Put a Roman numeral in front of each main idea—I., II., III. Then write a few supporting details under each main idea. Put a capital letter in front of each detail—A., B., C.

EXERCISE 1

Directions: Read this article that tells how computers have changed. Then complete the details in the outline.

How Computers Have Changed

Computers were a lot different 15 years ago than they are today. When computers were first built, they were so big that they filled a whole room. Computers were so expensive that only businesses could afford to buy them.

But now, as technology[1] has grown, computers have changed completely. Computers today are small enough to fit on a desk or on a person's lap. Computers today cost less than a family car, so many people have bought computers to use in their homes.

[1]Progress in the use of machines

Outline: How Computers Have Changed

I. What computers were like 15 years ago

    A. were so big that _____

    B. were so expensive that _____

II. What computers are like today

    A. are small enough that _____

    _____

    B. cost less than a car, so _____

    _____

(Answers are on page 120.)

MINDSTRETCHER

Some people who lived a hundred years ago predicted what things might be like in our world today. They guessed that people would be exploring the other planets, walking on the moon, and traveling in space cars above the crowded highways. They thought that robots would outsmart humans and that wars and diseases would no longer exist. Some of these predictions came true, and some did not.

Directions: Now it's your turn to make a few predictions. What will life be like in the year 2050?

1. How will people look and act?

    a) _____

    b) _____

2. Where will people be living?

    a) _____

    b) _____

3. How will people travel?

    a) _____

    b) _____

4. What other changes will there be?

    a) _____

    b) _____

(Answers will vary.)

Writing a Summary

When you finish reading an article, a good way to remember what you have read is to write a **summary**. When you summarize, you "sum up" the main idea of the article by writing it down in a few sentences in your own words. When you are studying for a test, you can read over your summary instead of rereading the whole article.

EXERCISE 2

Directions: Read this article. Then fill in the details that are missing from the outline.

Computers in the Future

In the future, computers will do many things for people at home. Computers will control televisions, lights, and alarm systems. Computers will help people do their shopping and banking without having to leave their homes.

In the future, computers will do many things for people at work. Computers will translate for people who are speaking different languages to each other on the phone. Computers will help people talk with each other while they are exchanging information on their computer screens. Computers will also help people do teleconferencing. Teleconferencing means that people will be linked by telephone, computers, and TV screens so that they can see each other while they are talking.

Outline: Computers in the Future

  I. Computers at home

    A. will control televisions, lights, and alarm systems

    B. _____

  II. Computers at work

    A. will translate for people who are speaking different languages to each other on the phone

    B. _____

    _____

    C. _____

Sample Summary: Computers in the Future

In the future, computers will do many things for people at home and at work. Computers will help people all over the world to communicate with each other more easily.

(Answers are on page 120.)

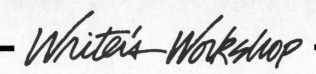

Directions: Complete each outline by writing details that would fit under each heading.

How Computers Affect Our Lives

  I. The good effects of computers on our lives

    A. _____

    B. _____

    C. _____

    D. _____

  II. The bad effects of computers on our lives

    A. _____

    B. _____

    C. _____

    D. _____

Books Serve a Purpose

  I. Reasons why authors write books

    A. _____

    B. _____

    C. _____

  II. Types of books people like to read

    A. _____

    B. _____

    C. _____

(Answers will vary.)

EXERCISE 3

Part A

Directions: As you read this article about robots, <u>underline</u> the topic sentence in each paragraph. Then write them in the outline. The main idea sentence has been underlined for you.

Robots Now and in the Future

<u>Robots are now doing many types of work in factories.</u> They are working on assembly lines, making TVs, and passing parts from a conveyor belt into boxes. Robots can hold tools so that they can do welding and spray painting. And robots are moving heavy objects from place to place.

Robots are saving companies a lot of money. They do not often make mistakes that have to be corrected. Robots do not get sick or have to take time off. Robots are not paid hourly wages and they are not paid for vacation time.

Robots will be used a lot more in the future. They will search the bottom of the sea for rare minerals. Robots will also be sent into space to take soil samples, work in space factories, and repair faulty spacecraft. Someday, robots may repair pipelines underwater for the navy.

Outline: Robots Now and in the Future

I. <u>Robots are now doing many types of work in factories.</u>

   A. They can make TVs and pass parts from conveyor belts to boxes.
   B. They can hold tools to do welding and spray painting.
   C. They can move heavy objects from place to place.

II. _____

   A. Robots do not often make mistakes that have to be corrected.
   B. Robots do not get sick or have to be paid for time off.
   C. Robots are not paid hourly wages and are not paid for vacation time.

III. _____

   A. Robots will search the bottom of the sea for rare minerals.
   B. Robots will take soil samples, work in space factories, and repair faulty spacecraft.
   C. Robots may repair pipelines underwater for the navy.

Part B

Directions: Reread the outline about what robots will do in the future. Then write a summary that tells the main idea of the article. Use the main ideas labeled I., II., and III.

Summary

_____

_____

_____

(Answers are on page 120.)

CHECK-UP

Directions: Think about what you have learned about outlines so far. Write your answers on the lines.

1. How are main ideas labeled in an outline?

_____

2. How are details labeled in an outline?

_____

3. Complete this outline with your own words.

Things I Will Do Tomorrow

   I. Things I will do at home tomorrow

   A. _____

   B. _____

   C. _____

II. Things I will do at work or at school tomorrow

   A. _____

   B. _____

   C. _____

(Answers are on page 120.)

Articles

GETTING READY
Now that you have learned about making an outline and writing a summary, you will use these skills as you read some longer articles about what the future may be like.

What will we be doing about exploring space 50 to 100 years from now? Would you like to go? Here's what some scientists predict.

The Future in Space

Directions: Read the article. Then fill in the outline.

In the late 1990s, NASA (the National Aeronautics and Space Administration) plans to build a space station to orbit the Earth. This space station will be called Spacelab. A space plane will carry heavy cargo of needed supplies to Spacelab. Then crews can stay in space for three months at a time. A lot can be done from these space stations that will benefit planet Earth. NASA also hopes to explore what can be learned by taking trips to the moon.

Spacelab

The weightless state in Spacelab will have many advantages. First, better parts can be made for computers and calculators than could be made on Earth. Second, better materials for miniature (tiny) electronic machines can be produced. Third, new vaccines and medicines can be prepared to help fight disease.

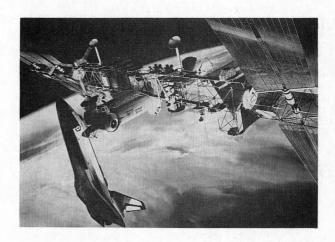

I. Advantages of weightlessness in Spacelab

   A. _____

      _____

   B. _____

      _____

   C. _____

      _____

How Spacelab Will Look

There are several things Spacelab will need to make it useful. Because there is no gravity, the walls in Spacelab will be lined with equipment to do experiments. Handrails will help scientists have a sense of "up" and "down." There will be a porthole with rails for looking at the stars and down at the planet Earth.

Trips to the Moon

Scientists will begin to explore the moon more fully for a few reasons. First, the surface of the moon is rich with silicon, used to make computer chips. Second, many metals like iron, aluminum, and magnesium, which Earth may run short of, are found on the moon. Third, moon rocks contain chemicals, which could help fuel rockets and boosters.

Moon Factories

Factories on the moon will be useful to Earth in many ways. Metals can be mined and purified in these factories. Spare parts can be made for orbiting space shuttles. Glass products, like optical fibers and lenses, can be made in these factories. Dangerous waste gases from these factories can be more safely gotten rid of on the moon so that Earth's atmosphere will become purer.

II. Things Spacelab will have to make it useful

    A. _____

       _____

    B. _____

       _____

    C. _____

       _____

III. _____

    A. _____

       _____

    B. _____

       _____

    C. _____

       _____

IV. _____

    A. _____

       _____

    B. _____

       _____

    C. _____

       _____

    D. _____

       _____

(Answers are on pages 120-121)

Do you know someone who has had laser surgery on his or her eyes? What other remarkable things are being done with lasers? Read this article to find out.

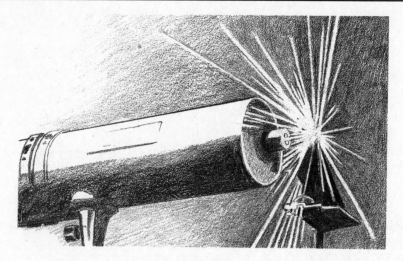

Lasers

Directions: Read the article. Then complete the outline.

History of Lasers

Many parts of our lives, from the most glorious (like trips through space) to the most ordinary (like weed killers for our lawns) will soon feel the impact of lasers. The first ruby laser was invented in New York City by Dr. Theodore Maiman. He used a piece of crystal to radiate energy that was hotter than the sun. This infrared energy is created by a series of rapid movements of atoms. Since then, lasers have been used for all kinds of useful purposes.

Medical Field

Lasers are now being used to weld a detached retina to a person's eye in a thousandth of a second, without pain or discomfort to the patient. Lasers are beginning to be used to treat skin diseases.

I. History of the first laser

A. _____
   _____

B. _____
   _____

C. _____
   _____

II. Ways lasers are being used in the medical field

A. _____

B. _____

Industry

In factories, lasers can cut and shape tough metals. Lasers can drill holes in hard surfaces without risk of breaking the materials. And lasers can weld different materials together, like metal to glass.

The Space Program

Lasers are being used to explore space. Since there is no atmosphere in space, lasers are being used in space satellite communication. Lasers can measure the distance from Earth to the moon within six inches. Lasers have been used to map the bottoms and rims of the moon's craters. Lasers can also monitor shock waves and rocket exhaust patterns.

Computers and Microfilm

Laser beams are being used in some computers because they can scan information in the speed of light. Lasers can also scan and locate a single word on a microfilm in a millionth of a second.

The Future

In the future, lasers may be used to produce instant fingerprint identification. Laser-powered rockets would reduce travel time greatly. And lasers may be used to heal wounds, mend broken bones, eliminate disease, and restore eyesight.

III. Ways lasers are being used by industry

A. _____

B. _____

C. _____

IV. Ways lasers are being used in the space program

A. _____

B. _____

C. _____

D. _____

V. Why lasers are being used in computers and microfilm

A. _____

B. _____

VI. Ways lasers may be used in the future

A. _____
_____

B. _____
_____

C. _____

D. _____

E. _____

F. _____

(Answers are on page 121.)

Writer's Workshop

Directions: Now that you have made an outline about how lasers will be used in the future, write a short summary, in your own words, telling the main idea of the article.

_____

_____

_____

_____

_____

_____

(Answers will vary.)

USING WHAT YOU'VE LEARNED

Directions: Scientists are looking for new ways of producing energy. They are looking for ways to harness the vast amounts of energy available from the sun, wind, earth, and sea. Check (✔) which types of energy you think may work best.

_____ **1.** solar heating panels on top of houses and buildings collect and store the heat from the sun

_____ **2.** geothermal (earth heat) power plants that convert heat from underground and volcanic rocks

_____ **3.** windmills with blades that can rotate at high speeds and operate electricity generators

_____ **4.** tidal power using a dam with turbines to produce electricity using the ebb and flow of the tide

_____ **5.** nuclear power to generate or produce electricity

(Answers will vary.)

Thinking ABOUT Thinking

When you make a prediction, you are making an educated guess. You are also giving an opinion.

Directions: Check (✔) which prediction in each set may come true in the distant future. Then give a reason for your choice.

☑ **A.** Someday, some people will live in space settlements.

☐ **B.** Even in the distant future, few people will live in space settlements.

As scientists and astronauts learn more and more about space,

it seems possible that some people will live in space settlements.

☐ **A.** By the year 2080, space satellites will supply the Earth with cheap, clean fuel.

☐ **B.** By the year 2080, sources of clean, cheap fuel will be found on Earth. Depending on space settlements will not be necessary.

☐ **A.** In the distant future, pollution will be so bad on Earth that people will die before they reach the age of 25.

☐ **B.** In the distant future, the sources of pollution will be dealt with. Humans will live comfortably on Earth, and the environment will be protected.

(Answers will vary.)

PASS IT ON

In this chapter you have learned some new information about the future in space and how lasers are being used now and may be used in the future.

Do yourself a favor. Pass on some new information you have learned. By telling someone else what you have learned, you will remember this information better.

1. What new information that you've learned in this chapter do you want to pass on?

_____

_____

_____

_____

_____

_____

_____

_____

_____

2. Who will you pass this information on to?

_____

_____

(Answers will vary.)

Answer Key

Chapter 1

EXERCISE 1
Pages 5-6

1. **a)** Washington
   b) Oregon
   c) California
   d) Hawaii
   e) Alaska
2. **a)** North America
   b) Australia
   c) Antarctica
   d) South America
   e) Africa
   f) Eurasia

EXERCISE 2
Page 7

1. nine planets in our solar system
2. three layers of Earth

Mindstretcher
Page 8

t j k p c r b v <u>t e n n i s</u> a z e r u q m x
e n p o q z d t x z c s y t r n a x b c c z
x r m a u p b n z <u>f o o t b a l l</u> u p p y k
z x m <u>s o c c e r</u> d b a m l z p m b n q a s

CHECK-UP
Page 8
Part A

1. Both have a topic and both have details.
2. A topic is a general idea that tells what a list or a paragraph is about.
3. A detail is a word or an idea that explains the topic.

Page 8
Part B

b

GETTING READY
Pages 9-10
Paragraph 1

b

Paragraph 2

a

Paragraph 3

a

Hawking's Physical Problems
Page 10

c) He can move only his eyes and three fingers.
d) He has difficulty swallowing liquids, and he cannot talk.
(Other answers are possible.)

Hawking's Daily Life
Page 11

c) Hawking communicates by using a computer.
d) He selects words, and the computer sends them to a voice machine.
(Other answers are possible.)

Big Bang Theory
Page 11

c) Twenty trillion years ago, matter and energy exploded.
d) It became the stars, planets, and everything else that is now the universe.
(Other answers are possible.)

Hawking's New Theory
Page 11

b) Hawking believes the universe is infinite.
(Other answers are possible.)

Thinking About Thinking
Page 12

1. **a)** yes
   b) fact
2. **a)** no
   b) opinion

Chapter 2

WARM-UP
Page 15
1. colors
2. jobs
3. books
4. music

EXERCISE 1
Page 16
1. places where people work
2. clothes
3. places where people live
4. languages

Mindstretcher
Page 16
1. birds
2. desserts
3. relatives
4. dogs

EXERCISE 2
Pages 17-18
Earmuffs
Topic sentence: At age 18, Chester Greenwood got a patent for his invention—earmuffs.

Page 18
Braille
Topic sentence: In 1824, at age 15, a blind French boy named Louis Braille invented a system so that blind people could read.

EXERCISE 3
Page 19
Roller Skates
¹ In 1863, James Plimpton of Massachusetts invented a pair of roller skates.
² He put rubber cushions between the foot plates and axles of a pair of shoes that had four wheels on the bottom.
³ The cushions allowed motion between the parts of the wheels.
⁴ The skater could shift his weight and use motion to steer.
⁵ Roller skating became a leisure activity.

CHECK-UP
Page 21
1. What is the paragraph about?
2. Topic sentence: There is an interesting story about how the first sandwich was created.
3. Topic sentence: See answer to number 2.
Details:
- fourth earl of Sandwich was a gambler
- he did not want to take time to eat
- during a card game, he ordered some meat and bread
- he slapped the meat and bread together
- he could eat with one hand and play cards with the other
- the sandwich became a very popular meal

GETTING READY
Pages 22-23
Potato Chips
Details:
- a guest complained about the french fries.
- George got angry and cut the potatoes into paper-thin slices
- he soaked the potatoes in water for 30 minutes, cooked them, and added salt
- he served the potatoes cold and crispy
- the customers loved the new treat

Iced Tea
Details:
- Richard Blychenden worked at the St. Louis Exposition as a tea salesman.
- the tea he tried to sell was too hot
- Richard poured the tea over ice
- hundreds of people came to his booth to try his iced tea

Cereal
Details:
- Drs. John and Will Kellogg ran a health clinic in Battle Creek, Michigan.
- they opened a food laboratory to test healthy new breakfast foods
- they wanted to create a low-starch, whole-grain wheat bread
- when they left the lab for several hours, the boiled wheat became soggy
- they pressed the wheat under flat rollers
- the wheat dried and broke up into separate flakes
- they poured milk over the flakes and called the new invention "cereal"

Looking at Inventions
Pages 24-25
Keeping a Light Bulb Glowing

Topic sentence: In 1879, Thomas Edison found a way to keep a light bulb glowing for a long period of time.

Details:
- he worked on this idea for 15 months
- he wanted to find the right filament (part that glows inside the bulb)
- he finally tried charred cotton thread, which glowed for 40 hours

Rubber Tires

Topic sentence: In 1839, Charles Goodyear was looking for a way to make rubber that could be used for tires.

Details:
- he mixed sulfur and white lead with gum rubber
- he found that the rubber was too soft and sticky in heat, and too hard and stiff in cold
- by accident, some of the mixture spilled onto a hot stove
- when the rubber cooled, it was tough and stayed the same in hot and cold temperatures
- he used this rubber to make the tires we use now

Penicillin

Topic sentence: In 1928, Alexander Fleming discovered penicillin by accident.

Details:
- he was studying bacteria and found mold growing on a culture
- he found that bacteria didn't grow in the culture with the mold
- he grew the mold in fluid and found it could kill common bacteria
- he tested the mold on mice, rabbits, and human cells
- Fleming called the medicine *penicillin*
- it was used during World War II to treat soldiers
- it is still used to fight bacteria

USING WHAT YOU'VE LEARNED
Page 26
Part A

1. b
2. d
3. a
4. c

Part B

3, 1, 4, 2, 5

Thinking About Thinking
Page 28
Part A

1. George Crum, Saratoga, New York, 1853
2. St. Louis Exposition, early 1900s
3. John and Will Kellogg, late 1800s
4. 1839, Charles Goodyear
5. Penicillin, Alexander Fleming, 1928

Page 28
Part B

1. better
2. most
3. best
4. everybody
5. all, more

Chapter 3

WARM-UP
Page 31

1. b, f
2. c, e
3. a, d

EXERCISE 1
Page 34

- A scientist discovered parts of a prehistoric female skeleton.
- Looking at the curve of her toe bones, the scientist could tell that Lucy had done some tree climbing.
- By rebuilding the missing parts of Lucy's skeleton, the scientist learned her height.
- Scientists are very excited that this skeleton has been found.

Mindstretcher
Page 35

1. a) TN   2. a) TN
   b) BT   b) TB
   c) TB   c) BT

EXERCISE 2
Pages 36-37

Scientists know a lot about the Neanderthals from studying their fossilized skulls, skeletons, and tools.

Writer's Workshop
Page 37
Possible answers:
Article 1: Primitive peoples made colorful cave paintings.
Article 2: Farming began thousands of years ago.

CHECK-UP
Page 38
1. topic sentence, detail sentences
2. main idea sentence, topic sentences, detail sentences
3. It tells what the article will be about
4. It sums up what has been stated in the article
5. Three Races of People
(Other answers are possible.)

GETTING READY
Page 39
Amazon Adventure
Main idea sentence: Dennis Werner had many questions about the Kayapo Indians before he met them.
Kayapo homes: a) mud houses with roofs made of woven palm leaves; **b)** houses built in a double circle around an open-air meeting place; **c)** snakes, rats, and bugs often came into the homes at night
Kayapo food: a) men hunt monkeys and wild pigs; **b)** men catch and eat fish; **c)** women have fruit and vegetable gardens; **d)** they grow sweet potatoes, bananas, pumpkins, and watermelons.
Kayapo games: a) do not keep score; **b)** no such thing as winning or losing; **c)** play to have fun and to try out skills.
Werner's feelings: a) the Kayapo became as familiar to him as friends at home; **b)** he came to love them as individuals.

Pages 41-42
Moving Away from the Stone Age
Main idea sentence: Throughout the past 12 thousand years, the way people have lived and worked has changed a lot as people's knowledge has grown.
Topic sentence: In the earliest times, men hunted large animals while the women and children gathered plants to eat.
Topic sentence: Much later, people became farmers and settled in one place.
Topic sentence: Gradually, people moved into small towns and villages and began trading and then buying and selling their goods.

USING WHAT YOU'VE LEARNED
Page 42
1. b
2. c
3. d
4. d
5. a

Thinking About Thinking
Page 43
Part A
1. Dennis Werner, 1984
2. 60 percent
3. 285
4. February 1976

Part B
1. think/believe/feel
2. think/believe/feel
3. opinion
4. seems

Chapter 4

WARM-UP
Page 47
Part B
correct order: 4, 1, 2, 3

EXERCISE 1
Page 47
correct order: 5, 1, 4, 2, 3

Mindstretcher
Page 48
Direction Set A
1. c
2. You might drown.

Direction Set B
3. d
4. an ice cream sundae

EXERCISE 2
Page 49
1940s—electric refrigerators
1950s—air conditioners and televisions
1980s—VCRs and computers

Writer's Workshop
Page 50
Part A

1. Peel the skins from the potatoes.
2. Cut the potatoes into long, thin slices.
3. Put oil in a frying pan and heat the oil.
4. Put the potatoes in the pan and fry them.
5. Enjoy the french fries.

Part B

Answers will vary.

EXERCISE 3
Page 51
The Bermuda Triangle

Underlined words are: 1492, a strange glow; 1872, a large sailing ship, the *Mary Celeste*, was found floating with no one on it; 1918, a large navy ship, the *Cyclops*, disappeared; 1973, another large ship, the *Anita*, was reported missing.

EXERCISE 4
Page 52

1. Before, During, After
2. First, Then, Finally
3. morning, noon, night

CHECK-UP
Page 53
Part A

1, 5, 2, 4, 3

Part B

Yesterday, Today, Tomorrow

GETTING READY
Pages 54-56
Dr. Martin Luther King, Jr.
Time Line

1955—organized peaceful sit-ins and demonstrations
1964–1965—the Civil Rights Act of 1964 was passed; awarded Nobel Peace Prize; Voting Rights Act of 1965 was passed
1968—April 4, King was shot and killed

Page 56

1. Black people did not have the same rights as white people.
2. Martin Luther King, Jr. Day is a national holiday so that Americans may honor a man of peace and vision.
3. Answers will vary.

Pages 57-59
Jane Addams
Time Line

1883—became social worker; visited settlement house in London
1889—opened Hull House in Chicago
1909—First president of National Conference of Charities and Corrections
1910—wrote *Twenty Years at Hull House*
1915-1929—president of Women's International League for Peace and Freedom; led fight for women's voting rights
1930—wrote *The Second Twenty Years at Hull House*
1931—awarded the Nobel Peace Prize
1935—died at age 75

Page 59

1. her visit to a London settlement house
2. **a)** a law was passed to limit required working hours to eight hours a day
   b) the first juvenile court was set up
   c) the first child labor law was passed
   d) housing reforms
3. Answers will vary.

Pages 60-63
Cesar Chavez
Time Line

1937—his family lost their 160-acre farm
1945—drafted into the navy
1948—married Helen Fabela
1951—met Fred Ross, organizer for CSO
1962—organized grape pickers; established the National Farm Workers Association
1966—union merged and called United Farm Workers Organizing Committee; national boycott against table grape growers
1970—union accepted; boycott ended
1973—organization renamed UFW; organized national boycott against lettuce growers

Page 62

1. The farm workers needed a union to fight for a decent rate of pay.
2. Answers will vary.

Thinking About Thinking
Page 64

1. F
2. O
3. O
4. F
5. F
6. O
7. O
8. F
9. F
10. O
11. F
12. O
13. F

USING WHAT YOU'VE LEARNED
Page 65

1. b
2. a
3. c

Chapter 5

WARM-UP
Page 67

1. same
2. different
3. same
4. different
5. different
6. 1, 3
7. 2, 4, 5

EXERCISE 1
Page 68

Part A

1. different
2. different
3. same
4. same
5. different

Page 69

Part B

Answers will vary.

EXERCISE 2
Page 70

Underlined words: more, also, both, compared with, for these reasons

Exercise 3
Page 71

Part A

alike, both, like, also

Part B

on the other hand/however, but, on the other hand/however

CHECK-UP
Page 72

1. same, different
2. Possible answers: see box on page 70
3. Possible answers: see box on page 70

GETTING READY
Pages 73-74
Day Care

Underlined words: both, both, however, unlike, on the other hand, while

1. **Possible answers:**
   Parents send children to day-care centers each day while they work.
   Day-care centers are staffed by trained teachers.
2. **Possible answers:**
   a) The French government pays for teacher training; the United States does not.
   b) The French government provides six hours of free day care for all 3–5 year-old children; the U.S. pays for day-care costs only for children of low-income families. French parents pay only $210 per year if they need more than six hours of day care a day; American parents often pay $200–400 per month.
3. Answers will vary.

Page 74-75
Medical Care

Underlined words: both, but, on the other hand, however, both, but

4. Great Britain has free health care for all; in the United States, some people have to pay out of their salaries for health insurance.
5. Answers will vary.
6. In the United States—not very long; in Great Britain—several months.
7. Possible answers: income, insurance, age

Pages 75-76
Recycling Garbage

Underlined words: both, while, but both

8. The United States—7 percent of its paper and glass; Japan—50 percent.
9. Poisoning of land and water can occur.
10. Earth Day, 1990
11. Answers will vary.

USING WHAT YOU'VE LEARNED
Page 76

1. d
2. b
3. a
4. c

Interview with Bob Harris about Japan
Pages 77-79

1. Both groups have kind, selfish, honest, and dishonest people.
2. Sometimes Japanese people will say yes when they mean no; they are not lying, however, but being polite.
3. Americans think of themselves as individuals. Japanese think of themselves as part of a bigger group.
4. as large families
5. Answers will vary.
6. Japanese children must take tests to see which schools they can enter. It is important for them to enter a good school so that they can get a good job afterward.
7. **a)** Most Japanese mothers do not work outside the home.
   b) Japanese fathers do not spend much time with their families because of work.
   c) Japanese fathers are obeyed.
8. Possible answers: crowded housing, high rents, few open spaces, few pension plans

Chapter 6

WARM-UP
Page 83

1. Since the movie was very funny, Gina laughed a lot.
2. The woman had a car accident; as a result her insurance rates went up.
3. After the man heard that his wife had triplets, he fainted.
4. Eva watered the plant almost every day; consequently, the plant grew large green leaves.
5. Because the music on the radio was playing so loudly, I didn't hear the doorbell ring.

EXERCISE 1
Pages 84-85

1. cause, effect, effect, cause
2. cause, effect, effect, cause
3. cause, effect, effect, cause

EXERCISE 2
Page 85

1. People receive improved medical care today.
2. Kids can play computer games, and adults can write letters and keep track of their bills.
3. The land has good soil.
4. People get less exercise, and they read less.

Mindstretcher
Page 87

1-3. Answers will vary.
   4. b

EXERCISE 3
Page 88
Part A

Underlined words reasons, why, because, so that, due to

a) They want to get an education before they have children.
b) They want to get their careers started first.
c) They want to save money before they have children.
d) Medical advances have made it safer for older women to have children.

Page 89
Part B

Underlined words: reasons why, because, so that, as a result

a) We now have very powerful monitors used in hospitals.
b) Microchips are now used in personal computers on Earth.

CHECK-UP
Page 89

1. cause, effect
2. **possible answers:** see box on page 88.

GETTING READY
Page 90-92
Fewer Factory Jobs

1. Yes. From 70–90% of all households have electricity, a radio, T.V., telephone, car, and washing machine.
2. **a)** People buy products made in other countries.
   b) U.S. companies are putting factories in countries such as Taiwan and Korea.
3. They believe that products made in other countries have better quality for lower prices.
4. **a)** science
   b) math
5. **a)** Workers go out of their way to learn new skills.
   b) Workers are encouraged to make suggestions to improve their factory's products.
6. Answers will vary.

Page 93
Father to Son

1. He knew he couldn't read or write well enough to do all the paperwork.
2. **a)** that he might break a machine
   b) that he might cause someone to get hurt
3. Answers will vary.

Pages 94-95
A Service Job in Your Future?

1. Factory workers make a product; service workers provide a service to others.
2. Service workers will not be well-paid unless they have a skill or special training.
3. **a)** Find out what jobs will be in demand.
   b) Select a job that meets your needs, interests, and abilities.
   c) Find and get training for the job you want.
4. **a)** the future of the job market
   b) your needs and interests
   c) where you can find the training
5. Answers will vary.

Thinking About Thinking
Page 97

1. Reason a
2. Reason b

Chapter 7

EXERCISE 1
Pages 100-101
How Computers Have Changed

  I. **A.** they filled a whole room
     B. only businesses could afford to buy them
  II. **A.** they can fit on a desk or a person's lap
     B. many people have bought computers to use in their homes

Exercise 2
Page 102
Computers in the Future

  I. **B.** will help people do their shopping and banking without having to leave their homes
  II. **B.** will help people talk with each other while they are exchanging information on their computer screens
     C. will help people do teleconferencing

EXERCISE 3
Pages 104-105
Robots Now and in the Future
Part A
Underlined topic sentences:
Robots are saving companies a lot of money.
Robots will be used a lot more in the future.

  II. Robots are saving companies a lot of money.
 III. Robots will be used a lot more in the future.
Part B
Answers will be similar to the following:
Robots are now doing many types of work in factories. They are also saving companies a lot of money. Robots will be used a lot more in the future.

CHECK-UP
Page 105

1. with Roman numerals
2. with capital letters
3. Answers will vary.

GETTING READY
Pages 106-107
The Future in Space

I.
- A. better parts can be made for computers and calculators than can be made on Earth
- B. better materials for miniature electronic machines can be produced
- C. new vaccines and medicines can be prepared to help fight disease

II.
- A. walls lined with equipment to do experiments
- B. handrails to help scientists have a sense of "up" and "down"
- C. a porthole with rails for looking at the stars and down at the planet Earth

III. Reasons scientists will begin to explore the moon more fully
- A. the surface of the moon is rich with silicon
- B. many metals that the Earth may run out of can be found on the moon
- C. Moon rocks contain chemicals which could help fuel rockets and boosters

IV. How factories on the moon will be useful
- A. metals can be mined and purified
- B. spare parts for orbiting space shuttles can be made
- C. glass products can be made
- D. dangerous waste gases will not pollute the Earth

Pages 108-109
Lasers

I.
- A. invented in New York City by Dr. Theodore Maiman
- B. He used a piece of crystal to radiate energy hotter than the sun.
- C. This infrared energy is created by a series of rapid movements of atoms.

II.
- A. to weld a detached retina to a person's eye in a thousandth of a second without pain
- B. to treat skin diseases

III.
- A. to cut and shape tough metals
- B. to drill holes in hard surfaces without risk of breaking the materials
- C. to weld together different materials

IV.
- A. in space satellite communication
- B. to measure the distance from Earth to the moon
- C. to map the bottoms and rims of the moon's craters
- D. to monitor shock waves and rocket exhaust patterns

V.
- A. because they can scan information at the speed of light
- B. because they can scan and locate a single word on microfilm in a millionth of a second

VI.
- A. to produce instant fingerprint identification
- B. to power rockets that could travel much faster than the ones we have now
- C. to heal wounds
- D. to mend broken bones
- E. to eliminate disease
- F. to restore eyesight